What Makes Life Worth Living

For Caroline

What Makes Life Worth Living

On Pharmacology

Bernard Stiegler

Translated by Daniel Ross

polity

First published in French as *Ce qui fait que la vie vaut la peine d'être vécue*
© Flammarion 2010

This English edition © Polity Press, 2013

Polity Press
65 Bridge Street
Cambridge CB2 1UR, UK

Polity Press
350 Main Street
Malden, MA 02148, USA

ISBN-13: 978-0-7456-6270-1
ISBN-13: 978-0-7456-6271-8(pb)

A catalogue record for this book is available from the British Library.

Typeset in 11 on 13 pt Sabon
by Toppan Best-set Premedia Limited

Printed and bound in Great Britain by MPG Books Group Limited, Bodmin, Cornwall

The publisher has used its best endeavours to ensure that the URLs for external websites referred to in this book are correct and active at the time of going to press. However, the publisher has no responsibility for the websites and can make no guarantee that a site will remain live or that the content is or will remain appropriate.

Every effort has been made to trace all copyright holders, but if any have been inadvertently overlooked the publisher will be pleased to include any necessary credits in any subsequent reprint or edition.

For further information on Polity, visit our website: www.politybooks.com

Contents

vi

Contents

Acknowledgements

The Publishers are grateful to the original publishers for permission to reproduce material (which runs in this edition from Section 2 of Chapter 1 to Section 23 of Chapter 2) included on pages 294–310 of the collection *Theory after 'Theory'*, edited by Jane Elliott and Derek Attridge and published by Taylor and Francis in 2011.

Sources for epigraphs are as follows: p. viii: Donald W. Winnicott, *Playing and Reality* (London: Routledge, 1971), p. 87; p. viii: Marcel Proust, *Days of Reading* (London: Penguin, 2009); p. 7: Jacques Derrida, *Of Spirit: Heidegger and the Question* (Chicago, IL, and London: University of Chicago Press, 1989), pp. 3–4; p. 101: Sigmund Freud, 'The Uncanny', *The Standard Edition of the Complete Psychological Works of Sigmund Freud*, vol. 17 (London: Hogarth Press, 1955), p. 226.

Do not be careless [*me amelesete*].

Socrates, in Plato, *Phaedo* 118a

Living itself [is a] therapy that makes sense.

Donald W. Winnicott, *Playing and Reality*

The supreme effort of the writer as of the artist only succeeds in partially raising for us the veil of ugliness and insignificance that leaves us uncaring [*incurieux*] before the world. Then, he says to us:

'Look, look
'Fragrant with clover and artemesia
'Holding tight their quick, narrow streams
'The lands of the Aisne and the Oise.'

Marcel Proust, *Days of Reading*

Consumers consume consumptions.

Raymond Queneau

Introduction

The loss of the feeling of existing

A mother, according to Donald Winnicott,[1] by taking care of her infant, even before the child is old enough to speak, teaches it that life is worth living. She instils in the child the *feeling* that life is worth living.

Maternal care, which obviously provides this feeling back to the mother herself, passes through the intermediary of what Winnicott called the 'transitional object'. This object enables and conditions the relation between mother and child and, as such, it is not a mere intermediary: it *constitutes* the mother as this mother, in her very way of being a mother, and this child as her child.

The transitional object has a distinct virtue: it does not exist. Certainly, something exists that enables it to appear – for example, a teddy bear or cuddly toy. But what makes this teddy bear or cuddly toy *able* to open up 'transitional space' – which Winnicott also called 'potential space' – in which the mother *can* encounter *her* child; what makes this teddy bear or cuddly toy able to become the transitional object, is that, beyond that part of the object that exists in external space, beyond or beneath this piece of cloth, there holds something that is precisely neither in exterior space, nor simply internal to either the mother or the child.

In this beyond or beneath of both the exterior and the interior, there is something that holds *between* the mother and her child, and which nevertheless does not exist. What takes hold between the mother and child in not existing, but in passing through the transitional object, and which therefore finds itself constituted by it, links and *attaches* them to one another through a wonderful relationship: a relation of love, of *amour fou*.

What holds and is upheld as this link through which these two beings become incommensurable and infinite for one another, is what, by allowing a place for that which is infinite, *consists* precisely to the *immeasurable extent* [*dans la mesure et la démesure*] *that it does not exist* – because the only things that exist are finite things.

This consistence, more than anything else, and before anything else, is what a mother protects when she protects her child. This protection, which is care par excellence, is grounded in the knowledge the mother has of the extra-ordinary character of the object – and that Winnicott calls transitional precisely in order to designate this extra-ordinariness.

Such was Winnicott's great discovery: the fact that maternal knowledge is *knowledge of that which, in the transitional object, consists, though it does not exist,* and which gives to the child placed under this protection the feeling that 'life is worth living'.[2]

I argue in this work that the transitional object is the first *pharmakon*.

The question of the *pharmakon* first arose in contemporary philosophy with Jacques Derrida's commentary on the *Phaedrus* in 'Plato's Pharmacy'.[3]

Writing – as *hypomnesis, hypomnematon,* that is, artificial memory – is that *pharmakon* whose artificial and poisonous effects Plato combats by opposing them to *anamnesis,* to thinking 'for oneself', that is, to the *autonomy* of thought. Derrida has shown, however, that this autonomy nevertheless always has something to do with heteronomy – in this case, that of writing – and that, while Plato *opposes* autonomy and heteronomy, they in fact constantly *compose*.

The transitional object is the first *pharmakon* because it is both an external object on which the mother and child are *dependent* (losing it is enough to make this clear) and in relation to which they are thus heteronomous; and an object that, not existing but consisting, provides (through this very consistence) sovereignty to both mother and child: their serenity, their trust in life, their feeling that life is worth living, their autonomy.

The *pharmakon* that is the transitional object is the point of departure for the formation of a healthy psychic apparatus. And it is also, in particular through sublimation, a condition of keeping the psychic apparatus of the adult in good health.

But Winnicott shows that a bad relation to this object and to its heteronomy is just as possible as the care that it alone makes possible. Dependence then becomes harmful, that is, destructive of autonomy and trust. The care that the mother must take of her child, then, necessarily includes the way she protects her child from this object: from what it contains that is threatening.[4] And eventually she must teach her children to detach themselves from it.

It is in this way that the mother must *bring* the child to *adopt* – or not – its *transitional situation*, that is, its *pharmacological situation*, on the basis of which the child will be *able* to attain, or not, the feeling that life is worth living. By bringing the child to adopt the *pharmakon*, what Winnicott calls the good mother also teaches the child to detach itself from the transitional object so as to engage with *other* transitional spaces, with which it will establish other relations, all of which may distance the child from the mother herself – despite which she does not lose her infinite dimension.

This is why the transitional object does not only concern the child and mother: it is also, as first *pharmakon*, the origin of works of art and, more generally, of the life of the mind or spirit in all its forms, and thus of adult life as such. It is, finally, the origin of *all* objects, because an object is always that which, once upon a time, appeared to a mind that *projected* it.

We shall see that, ultimately, *things* can constitute a *world* only insofar as they irreducibly proceed from the transitional character of the object. Having become ordinary and everyday, and in this sense 'mundane' (or 'intramundane'), the transitional object conserves its pharmacological dimension, even if this 'mundanity' tends to conceal this dimension. As such, it can always engage not only curative projection processes but poisonous ones, becoming, for example, the support of an addiction, the screen of melancholy, and even a drive of destruction, of murderous madness, of those dangerous states that result when the feeling that life is worth living has been lost.

To lose the feeling that life is worth living may drive one to furious madness.

Re-reading *Playing and Reality* over the last year in order to prepare a course which to some extent lies at the origin of the present work,[5] I was astounded to discover that, according to Winnicott, the patients under his care had 'lost the feeling of existing'. I was astounded because I immediately recalled that these were the exact words, 'lost the feeling of existing', that Richard Durn wrote in his diary when he admitted or forewarned, but a forewarning to no one in particular, that this loss was so abyssal and painful that it could well lead him to commit a massacre.[6]

The *pharmakon* is at once what *enables* care to be taken and that *of which* care must be taken – in the sense that it is necessary *to pay attention*: its power is *curative to the immeasurable extent* [*dans la mesure et la démesure*] that it is also *destructive*.

This 'at once' characterizes what I call a *pharmacology*, on which and from which I shall try to open perspectives in the pages which follow.

As far as I know, Derrida never envisaged the possibility of such a pharmacology – that is, of a discourse on the *pharmakon* understood *in the same gesture* in its curative and toxic dimensions. And this can only be a source of regret for *us*, those who, in the twenty-first century, are trying to remain non-inhuman beings, and for whom the question of the *pharmakon* is not merely an academic issue for learned philosophers: it obsesses each and every one of us.

This state of affairs [*état de fait*] requires a rule of law [*état de droit*], a thought that, even if it can no longer secure a clear separation between fact and right – a difference between heteronomy and autonomy that would be not only clear but absolute – nevertheless learns to distinguish them in a new way, that is, without opposing them. The pharmacological question that now concerns *each and every one of us* thus becomes a primary question *for the academic world and for the world as a whole*.

This pharmacological question haunts planetary consciousness and the planetary unconscious, just as it haunts the immense loss of trust that inevitably results from the loss of care. This question thus *characterizes* the economic and spiritual crisis afflicting the 'earth-ark'.[7] This crisis is therefore unprecedented, which means that it is more *critical* than ever.

Krisis means 'decision'. We all now know that it is the future of terrestrial life that is at stake with unprecedented urgency. We all know, whether we admit it or whether we prefer to know nothing about it, nor even to hear about it, that with the historical sequence that began to unfold in 2007, every step counts, and seems to be systemically overloaded with consequences that would be extremely difficult to reverse – if not absolutely irreversible.

It is in this context that there arises, today, the question of care, and of its condition: the *pharmakon*.

Part I

Pharmacology of Spirit

Is it not remarkable that this theme, spirit [...] should have been disinherited [*forclos d'héritage*]? No one wants anything to do with it any more, in the entire family of Heideggerians, be they the orthodox or the heretical, the neo-Heideggerians or the para-Heideggerians, the disciples or the experts. No one ever speaks of spirit in Heidegger. Not only this: even the anti-Heideggerian specialists take no interest in this thematics of spirit, not even to denounce it. Why?

Jacques Derrida, *Of Spirit: Heidegger and the Question*

1

Apocalypse Without God

1. Apocalyptic feeling and economic war

In 1919, Paul Valéry began '*La crise de l'esprit*' with the following words: 'We later civilizations...we too now know that we are mortal'.[1] *We too*, earthlings of the twenty-first century who have not been through a world war, and who form present-day human-kind, now know that we *are capable* of self-destruction. And if in the past the possibility of such an extinction of our kind was inconceivable other than as the consequence of God's anger – of original sin – today there is no longer any religious reference at the origin of this extreme global pessimism.

The cause of this mood, which became even more downbeat in 2009 after the collapse of the Copenhagen summit, is an economic war without mercy: a concealed conflict, a bottomless hypocrisy, a constant struggle, exhausting the Earth and its inhabitants, and leaving a billion of them in abominable economic misery while ruining the whole of the human world ever more quickly and ever more irreversibly, such that, in this war disguised as peace, it will not be long before everyone loses.

The name of this war is globalization – a globalization in which industrial technologies have become weapons that destroy ecosystems, social structures and psychic apparatuses. If the time has come for an armistice and, with it, for the negotiation of a new peace treaty, which would be a new contract, and not only a social

contract, but a scientific, technological and global contract; if too
many ruins are being accumulated in the name of 'development'
and economic competition, then this raises a preliminary question:
what relation to technics and to technologies would enable us to
think the reconstruction of a global future?

The economic crisis of 2007 and 2008 has exposed the profoundly destructive nature of the globalized industrial system.
Everybody now knows that it is no longer feasible to continue
pursuing the 'misgrowth' [*mécroissance*] that is a global economic
war disguised as a consumerist peace by the psycho-power of
marketing.[2] Yet nobody can see how to re-find the path capable
of leading to peaceful growth and development. It is this combination of knowledge and non-knowledge that leads to the spread of
this ordinary, everyday apocalyptic feeling – the feeling and the
knowledge that *something has come to an end*.

2. 'So many horrors could not have been possible without so many virtues'

In what he analysed in 1919 as a crisis *of mind or spirit*, Valéry
highlighted above all the *fundamental ambiguity* of this spirit – of
the science, reason, knowledge and even the moral elevation that
made possible so much ruination, death and devastation throughout Western Europe, beyond what any previous historical epoch
could ever have imagined:

> So many horrors could not have been possible without so many
> virtues. Doubtless, much science was needed to kill so many, to
> waste so much property, annihilate so many cities in so short a
> time; but *moral qualities* in like number were also needed.
> Knowledge and Duty, then, are suspect.[3]

Valéry, just like Husserl a little later, and like so many
thinkers who were overwhelmed between the wars, thus described
the way in which the First World War revealed that spirit is
always composed of two contrary sides: it is a kind of *pharmakon*
– *at once* a good *and* an evil, *at once* a remedy *and* a poison,
as Plato said about writing, which is the technology of the rational
mind.

The evidence for this pharmacology, for this ambiguity and hence for this fragility of spirit, impressed itself on Valéry and his contemporaries in the form of a series of interconnected crises – military, economic and spiritual[4] – through which science is 'dishonoured'.[5] After the First World War,

> everything essential in the world has been affected by the war [...]. *The Mind* [or Spirit] *itself has not been exempt from all this damage.* The mind is in fact cruelly stricken; it grieves in men of intellect, and looks sadly upon itself. It distrusts itself profoundly.[6]

3. 'Sciences of fact' and 'humanity of facts': the extinction of the Enlightenment

Sixteen years after Valéry, Husserl in turn spoke of a crisis of science. This crisis proceeds from a 'change which set in at the turn of the past century', which concerns 'the general evaluation of the sciences', and which aims at 'what science in general has meant and could mean for human existence':

> The exclusiveness with which the total world-view of modern man, in the second half of the nineteenth century, let itself be determined by the positive sciences and blinded by the 'prosperity' they produced, meant an indifferent turning-away from the questions which are decisive for a genuine humanity. Mere sciences of fact create a mere humanity of facts.[7]

At the time Husserl was writing these lines, Hitler had already been Chancellor for two years, and a plebiscite bestowing upon him the title of Führer had received support from 92 per cent of the German electorate.

> The change in public evaluation was unavoidable, especially after the war, and we know that it has gradually become a feeling of hostility among the younger generation. In our vital need – so we are told – this science has nothing to say to us. It excludes in principle precisely the questions which man, given over in our unhappy times to the most portentous upheavals, finds the most burning:

questions of the meaning or meaninglessness of the whole of this human existence.[8]

Reading these lines in 2010, how can we doubt that this malaise in relation to science has returned with even greater force? It is thus the spirit of the Enlightenment that seems to have been extinguished, writes Husserl. The Enlightenment – that is:

> the ardent desire for learning, the zeal for a philosophical reform of education and of all of humanity's social and political forms of existence, which makes that much-abused Age of Enlightenment so admirable.[9]

Having become 'positive sciences' and 'mere sciences of fact', and forming a 'mere humanity of facts', the Enlightenment has been inverted into Darkness. It has its hymn: 'We possess an undying testimony to this spirit in the glorious "Hymn to Joy" of Schiller and Beethoven.' But this hymn (which has become that of the European Union) can 'only with painful feelings [be heard] today. A greater contrast with our present situation is unthinkable.'[10]

4. Economy of spirit and organology

On the eve of the Second World War, four years after Husserl published *The Crisis of European Sciences and Transcendental Phenomenology*, from which the above words are taken, Valéry returns in 'Freedom of the Mind' to the state of the *krisis* of mind or spirit, and deplores having to do so:

> It is a sign of the times, and not a very good sign, that today it is not only necessary, but imperative to interest people's minds in the fate of the Mind [or Spirit] – that is, in their own fate.[11]

Returning to the question of Spirit in 1939 was an attempt to interest minds in their own fate and in the fate of Spirit, above all by highlighting that this proceeds from a spiritual *economy*[12] that cannot be considered in isolation from the *material* economy:[13] these two economies, which must be distinguished as that of the useful and the useless,[14] but which can never be separated, are products *of the same organs.*

Seventy years after Valéry returned to this question, seventy years after the onset of the Second World War, which brought horror at a level that would have been unimaginable to the Valéry of 1919, we must draw the consequences of the fact that two inseparable yet contradictory economies operate with the same organs: these two economies call for an organology, which is also a pharmacology, given that what an organ can accomplish in the material economy (that is, *negotium*) may be *contrary* to what this very same organ makes possible in the spiritual economy (that is, *otium*):[15]

> The same senses, the same muscles, the same limbs; more than that, the same types of signs, the same tokens of exchange, the same languages, the same modes of logic that function in the most indispensable actions of our life, all likewise figure in our most gratuitous, conventional, and extravagant actions.[16]

These two economies are always in a relation of conflict over values, because our species always lives on two planes at once, which are also two different scales of value: the plane of conservation, on which all living beings live, and a plane that exceeds this conservation:

> In short, man does not have two sets of equipment, he has only one; and sometimes it functions to maintain his life, his physiological rhythm, and sometimes it furnishes the illusions and labours of our *great adventure.*[17]

And our organs – physiological and artificial – are always simultaneously at the service of these two economies, developing in parallel: 'The same ship or rowboat brought merchandise and gods...ideas and methods'.[18] And for a very long time there was a 'parallel between the intellectual development and the commercial, industrial, and banking development of the Mediterranean and Rhine basins'.[19] This, however, is no longer the case:

> Culture, cultural changes, the value put on matters of the mind, the appraisal of its products, and the place we give to these in the

hierarchy of man's needs – we know now that, on the one hand, all this is related to the ease and the variety of exchanges of all sorts; on the other hand, it is strangely precarious.[20]

In 1939, Valéry claimed to share with many of his contemporaries the 'sense of a decline of intellect, a threat to culture, a twilight of the purer divinities, [a sensation that is] growing stronger and stronger in all those who can sense anything in the order of those higher values of which we are speaking [under the name of spirit]'.[21] Such a becoming, which leads to a 'fall in spirit value',[22] proceeds from a suicidal tendency: 'there is an element of suicide in the feverish and superficial life of the civilised world'.[23]

5. Perfecting organs and melancholy

Ten years earlier, and ten years after Valéry's first address, Freud, perceiving the mass regression that he had already reflected on in 1921 in *Massenpsychologie*, pointed out that 'present-day man does not feel happy', and becomes even less happy the more he comes to resemble a 'prosthetic god'.[24]

In this 'malaise' of culture and civilization, technics (prostheticity) plays an essential role because it is eminently pharmacological, particularly as the *system of artificial organs* it forms in the industrial age. After listing the benefits of industrial technical progress, which seem to bring those near to me even nearer, to protect my children from death, to prolong my own life,[25] and so on, he raises the contrary and systemic secondary effects of this progress:

> If there had been no railway to conquer distances, my child would never have left his native town and I should need no telephone to hear his voice; if travelling across the ocean by ship had not been introduced, my friend would not have embarked on his sea-voyage and should not need a cable to relieve my anxiety about him. What is the use of reducing infantile mortality when it is precisely that reduction which imposes the greatest restraint on us in the begetting of children [...]?[26]

Such a becoming is only possible because, in an essential and original way, 'man is perfecting his own organs'.[27]

In the course of this 'perfecting' (or improvement),[28] technics constantly compensates for a *default of being* (of which Valéry also speaks)[29] by *constantly bringing about a new default – always greater*, always more complex and *always less manageable* than the one that preceded it. This constant disadjustment induces frustrations, narcissistic wounds, and melancholy.

6. Pharmacology of the imagination

In *Dialectic of Enlightenment*,[30] five years after 'Freedom of the Mind', Adorno and Horkheimer emphasized how a diversion [*détournement*] of reason, or a reversal [*retournement*] of reason, reducing the project of the *Aufklärung* to rationalization,[31] led to the opposite of that reason which the *Aufklärer* conceived essentially as the emancipation of minds and the conquest of maturity [*majorité*], that is, as the struggle against minority.

Thus rationality becomes rationalization, in the sense given to this word by Max Weber, 'rationalizing' society by spreading the reign of calculability, and producing the opposite of maturity understood as the individual and collective formation and education of intelligence and knowledge, that is, understood as *Bildung*. And rationalization, which here appears as the application and *technical* diversion of scientific reason (which is precisely what Habermas maintained), engenders an immense social and psychic irrationality, that is, a massive alienation of mind and spirit.

This is what results from the fact that these minds have become, above all, consumers targeted by the culture industry, the control of minds driving them back into their minority, thereby completing what was begun with the submission of the bodies of producers to the service of machines, that is, completing their proletarianization. Such was the 'fall of spirit value' observed in America in 1944 by these two Germans who had emigrated to New York in order to re-establish the Institute of Social Research created in Frankfurt in 1932.

What such an analysis ignores, however, is the pharmacological character of technics in general, and of the psycho-technologies implemented by the culture industries in particular. It is on this precise point that there is a divergence between Adorno and

Benjamin (who committed suicide in 1940): whereas for Benjamin industrial technics, as the essential phenomenon of reproducibility, opens a new political question – imposing on philosophy a new task, new criteria of judgement, a new critique (a new analytic for the new perceptual possibilities arising with the organological turn constituted by the technologies of the reproducibility of the sensible) – for the thinkers of critical theory, this fact was, on the contrary, apprehended essentially and exclusively as a critical regression.

Habermas has drawn the consequences of this position by essentially defining rationalizing reason – that is, the power to dominate through rationalization (and to legitimate this domination by science-become-technoscience) – as rational activity in relation to an end, 'purposive-rational activity',[32] while he defines *technological rationality* essentially as the means to such an end, thereby opposing it to speech, which, as communicative activity, is not the means of thought so much as its element.[33] This position is completely different to Valéry's.

It is thus the question of the essentially pharmaco-logical (because techno-logical) character of *logos* itself that is ignored by Adorno and Horkheimer – and subsequently by Habermas. And this is because so-called critical theory proceeds with the Kantian transcendental imagination, just as Plato proceeds with the question of *anamnesis* in its relation to *hypomnesis*.

This 'critique' of the culture industry consists in effect and above all in denouncing, in the domination of Hollywood – and its development through television, which was then still to come – a teratology whereby that which constitutes the imagination as such, namely, what was conceptualized by Kant as the schematism of the *transcendental* imagination, finds itself mechanically expropriated by the cinematic system of production and projection: that is, by an *artificial* imagination which extenuates and atrophies the transcendental imagination, just as *hypomnesis* bypasses, short-circuits and annihilates the *anamnesis* that, for Plato, defines thought itself.

Now, just as the literal (that is, lettered) *pharmakon* is the condition of its own critique,[34] the transcendental imagination and its schema will always already have necessitated a cinema of projections founded on repro-ducibility, which is the condition of possibility (and impossibility) of what Kant called the *synthesis speciosa*, that is, the capacity for figuration.[35]

As rational imagination, the transcendental imagination of which the *synthesis speciosa* is the projection must retain the trace of what it imagines by putting it into images – and geometry as figuration is essentially *this* experience, foundational for all philosophy, into which it is impossible to enter without having experienced the pharmacology of the figure, that is, of the imagination. Such is the challenge of *The Origin of Geometry*.[36]

This figure can in fact always present itself as a disfiguration [*défiguration*], since the geometrical concept could never be reduced to the configuration of a figure that would inevitably be empirical, that is, artificial [*factice*]: it is geometrical only as a figure that supports a reasoning that it projects, a reason that sublimates and idealizes it, that projects a mathematical ideality. Kant proposes that this ideality pre-cedes, as concept, its projection into figure, a concept that might thus be said to be a priori, whereas it is always possible to make a posteriori use of such a figure *without* geometrical knowledge, and in the service of a technical knowledge, that is, of a knowledge that is blind to it.

It is in this way that the mason is able to make use of a geometrical rule that he has not himself thought – that he does not himself understand. And this can, according to Husserl, generate a technicization of scientific institutions and an automation of calculation, such that the European sciences enter into crisis because they have lost their 'originary intuitions'.[37]

Kant, however, opposes the schema (that is, the concept) to the image, and proposes that the image always presupposes the schema, which would therefore be the transcendental origin – the image being only an empirical translation of the transcendental faculty that is the imagination as such. In so doing, Kant makes it impossible to think the originarily pharmacological condition of the imagination, which, contrary to his analyses, always presupposes its projection through a technical exteriorization[38] in an object-image, which is what I call 'tertiary retention'.[39]

7. Anamnesis and transindividuation

Whether it is a matter of the critique of sophistic logography according to Plato, or the critique of Hollywood's artificial imagination according to Adorno and Horkheimer, what is at stake is the relation to the *pharmakon*, that is, to technics. But Adorno and Horkheimer fail to understand technics pharmacologically – or else they see in the *pharmakon* only its poisonous character, which means that they do not see it *as pharmakon*.

Furthermore, in the twentieth century this 'pharmacology' that is technics became industrial, which is also to say, technoscientific: as rationalization, the *pharmakon* is now constituted *through science itself*, and it is as such a product of *anamnesis* – except that we may wonder whether, today, science remains anamnesic (this was precisely Husserl's question in *Crisis of the European Sciences*).[40]

Anamnesic memory, which for Plato was the source of all knowledge, all ontologically grounded *episteme*, all *mathesis* and all learning [*apprentissage*], constitutes the pure autonomy of thinking for oneself. As such, it could be called transcendental memory. Plato constituted this transcendental memory by opposing it to hypomnesic memory, that is, artificial memory, the *pharmakon*. Likewise, Kant devalued the object-image by subordinating it to the scheme, which he thus postulated as a transcendental absolute (an a priori concept) grounding an ontology.

Logos is always a *dia-logos* within which those who enter the dialogue co-individuate themselves – trans-form themselves, *learn* something – by dia-loguing. This co-individuation can result in discord, in which case each participant is individuated *with* the other, but *against* the other – as occurs, for example, in a game of tennis or chess. But co-individuation can also result in accord or agreement, in which case it enables the *production of a concept* that is shared by the interlocutors, who thus together produce a *new locution* through which they agree on a meaning [*signification*] – which, in Platonic doctrine, must be produced in the form of a *definition* responding to the question, '*ti esti?*'[41]

In the terminology of Simondon, this meaning constitutes the 'transindividual'. The transindividual is the outcome of what I analyse as a process of transindividuation, in which circuits of transindividuation are produced, circuits that form networks, that are more or less long, through which intensities circulate (desires: circuits of transindividuation are always circuits of desire),[42] and which can be short-circuited.

An *anamnesic circuit* is a *long circuit co-produced by those through whom it passes*:[43] this is what Plato called 'thinking for oneself', and only in this way may a *mathesis* be formed into an *episteme*.

A hypomnesic circuit may bypass or short-circuit this long circuit through which a soul is trans-formed and through which it learns. It may come to de-form the soul as a consequence of interiorizing a circuit that it has not itself produced – by requiring the soul to *adapt* itself to a *doxa*, that is, to dominant ideas that have not been produced and conceived by those who merely submit to them, rather than share in them.

8. *Pharmakon, pharmakos* and the pharmacology of the scapegoat

It was Jacques Derrida who opened up the question of pharmacology – within which the hypomnesic appears as that which constitutes the *condition* of the anamnesic. I have striven in various works to establish how the noetic movements through which a soul is trans-formed are always arrangements of primary and secondary retentions and protentions, arrangements themselves conditioned by tertiary retentions, that is, by hypomnesic systems. It follows from these analyses that everything that *opposes* the anamnesic to the hypomnesic, such as transcendental memory or transcendental imagination, leads to an impasse.[44]

The fact remains that there is an historical and political necessity at the origin of such oppositions: Plato struggles against that sophistic that had caused the spirit of the Greek *polis* to enter into crisis through its misuse of the *pharmakon* – through bypassing and short-circuiting thought, that is, anamnesis, thus depriving the souls of citizens of that knowledge lying at the foundation of all citizenship (all autonomy). In this regard, the *pharmakon* was a factor in the proletarianization of spirit (in the loss of knowledge) just as the machine-tool would later be a factor in the proletarianization of the bodies of producers, that is, of workers (depriving

them of their know-how, their *savoir-faire*).[45] Likewise, it is a
system that proletarianizes minds that Adorno and Horkheimer
denounced in the Hollywood imagination machinery of the citi-
zen-become-consumer (even though they did not analyse it in these
terms).

Nothing is more legitimate than these philosophical struggles
against what, in technics or technology, is toxic for the life of the
mind or spirit. But faced with that which, in the *pharmakon*,
constitutes the possibility of a weakening of the spirit, these struggles ignore the originarily pharmaco-logical constitution of this
spirit *itself*. They ignore the *pharmacology of spirit* by taking the
pharmakon in general as a *pharmakos*: a scapegoat – like those
found in the sacrificial practices of polytheistic ancient Greece, or
equally in Judea, practices in which this *pharmakos* is laden
[*chargé*], as Christ will be, with every fault, before being led 'into
an inaccessible region'.[46]

9.   Pharmacology of the transitional object and default of interiority

What would be regressive, here, would be to propose that tertiary
retention is a poison that destroys interiority, because in fact there
never was any interiority – if by that is meant an originally virgin
source of all affection. Interiority is constituted *through the internalization* of a *transitional* exteriority that precedes it, and this is
as true for anthropogenesis as it is for infantile psychogenesis: *the
transitional object constitutes the infantile stage of the pharmacology of spirit*, the matrix through which transitional space is formed
in transductive relation to the 'good mother', that is, to the pro-
vider of care.

This relation of care constituted by the transitional object, that
is, by the first *pharmakon*, forms the basis of what becomes, as
transitional space, an intermediate area of experience where
objects of culture, the arts, religion and science are formed:

> Of every individual that has reached the stage of being a unit with
> a limiting membrane and an outside and an inside, it can be said
> that there is an *inner reality* [...] but is it enough? [T]he third part
> of the life of a human being, a part that we cannot ignore, is an

intermediate area of *experiencing*, to which inner reality and external life both contribute.[47]

Spirit is the *après-coup* internalization of this non-interiority (as
revenance), also referred to by Winnicott as 'potential space',[48]
and this internalization presupposes care, that is, a process of
apprenticeship through which an art of internalization is developed – an art of living – that Winnicott called creativity.

Within that pharmacological space that is 'potential space',
which alone makes this creativity possible, where *pharmaka* form
transitional objects of all kinds, autonomy is not what *opposes*
heteronomy, but that which *adopts* it as a necessary default [*un
défaut qu'il faut*], and is what 'makes the individual feel that life
is worth living'.[49] What Winnicott called the self ('the interior') is
constituted from the *primordial default of interiority* as the adoption (as creativity, that is, as individuation) of transitional space.
Internalization is a co-individuation of this space itself (transitional space thus being constituted as a process of transindividuation in which circuits form).

Pharmacologically, transitional space becomes poisonous (that
is, in the language of Winnicott, a form of 'illness')[50] when it
installs

> a relationship to external reality which is one of compliance, the
> world and its details being recognised but only as something to be
> fitted in with or demanding adaptation. Compliance carries with it
> a sense of futility for the individual and is associated with the idea
> that nothing matters.[51]

The thought of non-interiority is without doubt what, in a thousand ways, characterizes philosophical thought in the twentieth
century, in Europe as in America, but also, as we have just seen,
and in an essential area, in psychopathology. There is no doubt that
this constitutes the common ground of so-called 'French theory'.
What, however, remains at worst ignored, but at best a site that has
hardly been opened – which thus constitutes, and this is my thesis,
the major site on which to build a *new critique* – is the pharmacological and therapeutic question constituted by the transitional
space of those transitional objects that are *pharmaka*.

This site remains *hardly* [*à peine*] opened because pharmacology presupposes organology, itself including and necessitating a history of the process of grammatization[52] (which grammatology, as logic of the supplement, was insufficient for thinking).

10.   The pharmacological critique of the unconscious

If this is the precise point on which 'critical theory' remains unsatisfactory, in lacking what constitutes the condition of any critique (of which anamnesis is for Plato the model), namely, the *pharmakon*, which *also* makes possible the short-circuit of any critique, it nonetheless remains the case that in *Dialectic of Enlightenment* Adorno and Horkheimer succeeded in identifying the unfolding of a process in which the culture industries become the central element. And it remains necessary in our time to reopen this question by honouring the lucidity of these thinkers, as well as certain others – and in particular Marcuse[53] – while nevertheless analysing their limits (which is the only way of honouring a philosophy).

To analyse their limits is to lose oneself in, and to try and feel one's way around in, shadows: in what their illuminations *owe* to shadows, if it is true that lucidity is that which brings light, and if it is true that there is no light without shadows – if not blindness. This task arises today, as ever, and as the reopening of the question of reason, at the very moment when rationalization, and the resulting domination of the irrational, now constitutes a systemic stupidity [*bêtise*][54] – lying at the heart of what must above all be described and delimited as a systemic crisis of global finance.[55]

Systemic stupidity is engendered by *generalized proletarianization*, from which there is no escape for *any* actor within the consumerist industrial system,[56] proletarianization resulting precisely from a pharmacological development, where the *pharmakon* short-circuits those whom it inscribes in the circuit of production, consumption and speculation, and does so by destroying *investment, that is, the desiring projection of imagination.*[57]

The real question is not, however, as Adorno and Horkheimer believed, the *exteriorization of imagination* (there has *never* been any imagination *without* object-images, that is, without tertiary retentions of all kinds), but rather the *dysfunction of that libidinal economy* that is presupposed by reason, reason being a fruit of a libidinal economy that constitutes it as *projector of shadows as well as light* – of powers and potentials of the unconscious constituting the depth of field of consciousness.

Revisiting the questions of critical theory, a new critique is required by the originarily pharmacological situation of spirit: a pharmacological critique *of the unconscious* – and here this clearly involves a double genitive. If reason has always been *opposed* to passion, to *pathos*, both of these themselves confounded with affect and desire, nevertheless for Plato (in *Symposium*) desire is the condition and the *necessary default* [*le défaut qu'il faut*] of philosophy. And for Aristotle, whose *On the Soul* is the horizon of Spinoza's *Ethics*, desire (as movement towards the prime unmoving mover, object of all desire) is the condition of all forms of life: vegetative, sensitive or noetic.

What still lies before us, when it comes to reason understood above all as motive, as the most elevated modality of desire (that is, of movement, of e-motion), is to identify the role of *pharmaka* in the formation of desire in general, and in the formation of reason in particular – in the formation of consciousness as attention, in the sense both of psychic attention and social attention, that is, moral consciousness – such that it then constitutes the therapeutic of this pharmacology.[58]

This is the point of departure for a new critique, which is necessarily as such a critique of the unconscious: the *pharmakon*, in all its forms, is above all a support for the projection of fantasies, that is, a sort of fetish. As such, it is always possible for it to cause desire to regress to a purely drive-based stage. From out of the critique of the unconscious, and as *practice* of the *pharmakon* as a transitional object, a new critique of consciousness becomes possible, a new theory that can only be a *political economy of the spirit* as the formation of attention, itself conditioned by the play of primary and secondary retentions, a play of retentions that the *pharmakon*, as tertiary retention, authorizes.

11.   Pharmacology of the libido

The fire of Prometheus is *at once*:

- the fire of Hephaestus, symbol of technical knowledge, but also of the fabrication of arms, which thus also brings the destructive fire of war; and
- the fire of desire that takes care of its object, but that is always close to the burning drives, source of consumption in all its forms.

The fire of Prometheus, symbol of both desire and technics, is therefore the subject par excellence of the pharmacology of the unconscious, that is, of the libido.

Vernant outlined the elements of a pharmacology of fire that is simultaneously that of technics (Hephaestus and Prometheus), of desire (Pandora), and of domestic space, that is, of the most intimate *oikonomia* (Hestia, goddess of the hearth, of private space, of inside, forming a couple with Hermes, god of outdoors and of public space).[59] Hestia is the divinity of domesticity understood as the care taken of this *pharmakon* that is fire, and in this pharmacology that is, therefore, all economy – the ideal figure of a 'philosophy of care'.

Fire is the *pharmakon* par excellence. As civilizing process, it is constantly at risk of setting fire to civilization. As the emblem common to technics and desire, it constitutes and articulates a *dual logic of the necessary default*:

- that logic shown by Freud to operate via the 'perfecting of organs', that is, as technics, a process that interminably *displaces* organic and organological default, that default that is necessary; and
- that logic that Lacan attempted to describe as 'lack' – which is *precisely not a mere lack*, but on the contrary *necessary*: the stoic quasi-cause.[60]

Technics, which thus pharmacologically constitutes the default insofar as it forms the horizon of desire, simultaneously opens two antagonistic yet inseparable paths: that of the drives, and that of sublimation.

In other words, the *two tendencies* of the *pharmakon* are the *two tendencies of libidinal economy*: these are, pharmacologically, when on the one hand it produces long circuits through which it becomes care, entering into the service of the libido orientated through sublimation; and when on the other hand it produces short-circuits, and is thus submitted to the drives, short-circuiting and bypassing sublimation, that is, the binding of the drives. Long circuits connect or bind the drives that are disconnected or unbound by short-circuits (Hephaestus, from whom Prometheus stole fire for mortals, is a 'god of linkages').[61]

It is the *play* of Eros and Thanatos that is instituted by this pharmacology. That which is pharmacological is always dedicated to uncertainty and ambiguity, and thus the prosthetic being is both ludic and melancholy: it is 'made of bile'. The liver of Prometheus that is devoured by the eagle, that continuously re-grows like an organic 'perfecting' without end, links technics not only to desire but to death, and to its anticipation. It is between Eros and Thanatos that what Hesiod called *elpis* is tied (*attente*, to await, to expect, that is, *attention*, care, protention, both as hope and as anxiety).[62] Mortals, for whom *elpis* – condition of what Heidegger called *Sorge* and *Besorgen*, the care and calculation of concern [*préoccupation*] – is as ambiguous as the *pharmakon*, must constantly *care for* their melancholy.

And just as melancholy is essentially the fact of dependence, as Freud teaches,[63] so too the *pharmakon* becomes a poison when it provokes dependence – heteronomy, that is, loss of *autonomia*, as *Phaedrus* says: atrophied by writing, memory can no longer go without its *hypomnematon*. But, as we shall see, there is no autonomy other than as the *adoption* of heteronomy, that is, of a *pharmakon*, so that dependence opens a milieu – that milieu that Winnicott called transitional space.

A letter from Freud to Fliess indicates that addiction is originally inscribed in libidinal economy.[64] Wherever there is dependence and addiction, there is a pharmacological situation that makes it possible – the loved one is only constituted as object of desire by themselves becoming a kind of *pharmakon* surrounded by *pharmaka* that are fetishized objects. Nevertheless, 'most mothers allow their infants some special object and expect them to become, as it were, addicted to such objects'.[65]

12.   Socrates and Asclepius

If the poisonous and addictogenic character of the *pharmakon* is its deficiency [*défaut*], the becoming-remedy of this *pharmakon* occurs when this deficiency is inverted, becoming that which is necessary, the necessity for poison to become virtue, of which the snake entwined around the rod of Asclepius is the emblem.

At the very end of *Phaedo*, in his final moments, Socrates asks Crito to sacrifice a rooster on his behalf to this mortal-become-god:

> Crito, we ought to offer a cock to Asclepius. See to it, and do not forget [*kai me amelesete*].[66]
>
> No, it shall be done, said Crito. Are you sure that there is nothing else? Socrates made no reply to this question, but after a little while he stirred, and when the man uncovered him, his eyes were fixed. When Crito saw this, he closed the mouth and eyes.[67]

Socrates, having drunk the hemlock, thereby honoured the god of poison and of cure:

> Asclepius was entrusted by his father to the centaur Chiron, who taught him medicine. And soon Asclepius became somebody of great skill in this art. He even discovered the means to revive the dead. In fact, he had received from Athena the blood which had flowed through the veins of the Gorgon; while the veins of the left side had spread a violent poison, the blood of the right side was beneficial, and Asclepius knew how to use it to restore life to the dead. [...] Zeus, confronted by these resurrections, believed that Asclepius had overturned the order of the world, and struck him down.[68]

2

Pathogenesis, Normativity and the 'Infidelity of the Milieu'

13. Anthropogenesis as pathogenesis

Rationalization, as first described by Weber, then by Adorno and Horkheimer, subjects all circuits of transindividuation to *pharmaka* of biopower and psychopower. Rationalization thereby destroys reason as desire, because it essentially consists in a process of generalized proletarianization, that is, of disindividuation, through the spread of short-circuits. It thus installs a pharmacological situation leading to generalized addiction, as a result of which, today, consumption has become a source of unhappiness.

Contemporary apocalyptic feeling essentially derives from this addictive turn. It is in this context that the Association nationale des intervenants en toxicologie et en addictologie decided that its 2009 conference would take as its theme, 'addictogenic society'. In such a society, where consumerism is taken to its ultimate limit, pathology stands in a completely new relation to desire such as it is constituted by the *pharmakon*:[1] a relation in which its drive-based tendencies are systematically exploited while its sublimatory tendencies are systematically short-circuited, in such a way that *pathos* has essentially become poisonous.

Pathos is affection in general, both as *bond* and as *illness*.

In the form of technical life proper to noetic souls, *pathos* – or what is referred to as *philia, eros, agape* or fraternity, names

referring to the *patho-logical condition of social life* – passes in
an original and essential way through the *pharmakon* that is
intrinsically pathogenic: anthropogenesis must be understood as
pathogenesis to the strict extent that it is technogenesis.

The pharmacological consideration of technics leads to a *patho-genetic* concept of *anthropos* in which pathology must be thought
on the basis of what Canguilhem called the 'normativity of the
living'. Life is a process and, in the course of life, life-forms
stabilize themselves.[2] Within this process, the specific life-form
that appears with humanity is characterized by a variability that
induces the appearance of artificial organs within the vital process:

> Bichat said that animals inhabit the world while plants are tied to
> their place of origin. This is even truer of human beings than of
> animals. [Man] is the animal who, through technics, succeeds in
> varying even his ambient surroundings [that is, the world environ-
> ment, the *Umwelt*] of his activity. Man thereby reveals himself to
> be currently the only species capable of variation. Is it absurd to
> assume that in the long run man's natural organs may express the
> influence of the artificial organs through which he has multiplied
> and continues to multiply the power of the former?[3]

For humans the normal, the pathological and normativity all
stand in an essential relation to artificial organs (Canguilhem thus
placed the Freudian question of the 'perfecting of organs' at the
heart of this patho-anthropology):

> Man, even physical man, is not limited to his organism. Having
> extended his organs by means of tools, man sees in his body only
> the means to all possible means of action. Thus, in order to discern
> what is normal or pathological for the body itself, one must look
> beyond the body. [...] From the moment mankind technically
> enlarged its means of locomotion, to feel abnormal is to realise that
> certain activities, which have become a need and an ideal, are
> inaccessible.[4]

The normal and the pathological are not in opposition. 'The
pathological is a kind of normal', and in the experience of the
pathological, life is normative: it invents states of health – inventions that Canguilhem described as the institution of new norms:

Being healthy means being not only normal in a given situation but also normative in this and other eventual situations. What characterizes health is the possibility of surpassing the norm, which defines the momentary normal, the possibility of tolerating infractions of the usual norm and of instituting new norms in new situations.[5]

A constant problem for readers of *The Normal and the Pathological* is to know which propositions refer to all living things, and which refer specifically to human life. Be that as it may, life that has been technically extended opens up a new experience of the pathological and thus of normativity.

Broadly speaking, the health of life as variability or changeability is the experience of the 'infidelities' of its milieu: 'Health is a margin of tolerance for the infidelities [*infidélités*] of the environment [*milieu*]'.[6] '[T]he environment is inconstant [*infidèle*]. Its infidelity is simply its becoming, its history.'[7] This infidelity or unreliability of the milieu is related to what Bertrand Gille called 'disadjustment' in order to designate gaps between the constantly accelerating evolution of the technical system (particularly since the Industrial Revolution) and that of the other human systems – social systems and psychic systems – all of which must also be thought in relation to natural systems (geographical, geological, meteorological, biological and physiological).[8]

From this perspective, technicity must be understood as bringing about a new 'infidelity' of the milieu – and of a milieu that is neither internal nor external, *a milieu of transitional objects* – that is, a changeability where the normal, the pathological and normativity develop according to a new logic. It is only within this new organological context, insofar as it constitutes a pharmacological context and is, as such, newly pathogenic, that Canguilhem can conclude: 'Man feels in good health – which is health itself – only when he feels more than normal.'[9]

The health of the pharmacological being is therefore an excess. But there is no excess that does not derive from a deficiency, a default – no more than there is any excess that does not cause a default. As such, this excess is both what derives from a disadjustment and what induces a disadjustment, because it exceeds the normal, *exceeds* the fact of being 'adapted to the milieu and its exigencies'.[10]

This primordial inadequation, which Simondon analysed as the phase difference of the individual in relation to their pre-individual milieu, that is, their relation to themselves insofar as they are a processual being inseparable from their associated milieu, is also what for Winnicott constitutes creativity – which I follow Simondon in calling 'individuation'.

The healthy human being is creative, according to Winnicott[11] – that is, as Canguilhem wrote, 'normative, capable of following new norms of life'.[12] And Canguilhem concludes with extraordinary audacity: 'the power and temptation to fall sick are an essential characteristic of human physiology'.[13]

There is no better way to say that pathogenesis is essential to anthropogenesis – which is itself a technogenesis of *pharmaka*. It is to this immeasurable extent that Thérèse Brosse could write that 'the problem of functional pathology seems to be intimately tied to that of education. The consequence of a sensory, active, emotional education, if it is done badly or not at all, is to instantly call out for re-education'.[14]

14. Proletarianization as disapprenticeship and the sterilization of pathogenesis

Apocalyptic feelings derive fundamentally from generalized proletarianization, which has led to a global loss of knowledge of all kinds: a massive process of *disapprenticeship* or *unlearning* [*désapprentissage*] on a planetary scale, imposing an adaptive society that is inevitably becoming addictive (spreading the heteronomic tendency of the *pharmakon*) and thus annihilating 'spirit value'.

This *loss of knowledge* has been felt above all and in various ways in the 'cultural' sphere, leading to various reactions, ranging from France's 'cultural exception' measures and international declarations protecting 'cultural diversity', to nationalist conflicts, sectarian fundamentalism and terrorism. Nevertheless, on the one hand, this loss of knowledge cannot be reduced to its cultural and religious aspects, while, on the other hand, it is yet to be correctly analysed – it has, ultimately, been to a very large extent underestimated.

It is not simply that cultural particularities have been lost, becoming either objects for heritage museums or for the curiosity of tourists (that is, objects integrated into the methods of marketing), or symbols of struggles for so-called 'identity': it is also the most elementary *savoir-vivre*, and *savoir-faire* in the form of arts and skills [*métiers*], that are being dissolved, along with the academic and universalist forms of knowledge that result from processes of anamnesic transindividuation. The regression of local *savoir-vivre* and *savoir-faire* never leads to the progression of universal knowledge: it always results in the complete opposite. It is this threefold deficit of knowledge that is referred to here with the term 'disapprenticeship' – which is a regression into minority in the Kantian sense.[15]

Far from extending the range of universal knowledge – if by 'universal' we mean a knowledge that has been *internalized as such*, that is, through the experience of the circuit of transindividuation that *constitutes* it as such, and at the origin of which lies an experience falling under what Plato called *anamnesis*, which, I argue, aims at a consistence – the destruction of local knowledge engendered by the standardization of ways of life has on the contrary entailed the destruction of curricular institutions charged with the formation and training of long circuits constitutive of disciplines and universal knowledge, that is, theoretical knowledge.[16]

It was inevitable that this situation would incite apocalyptic feelings: a pharmacological being that has become ultra-powerful while at the same time becoming acephalous and uncultivated could only be experienced as a blind power and an immense danger to itself and everything around it.

This situation was induced by a mutation of the *pharmakon* that, having become industrial, has become totally autonomous in relation to the therapeutic knowledge that constitutes social systems (in the sense of both Bertrand Gille and Niklas Luhmann): the infidelity of the 'technical milieu' has reached the point that it makes impossible the metastabilization of a psychosocial normativity and its transmission by that education that Brosse teaches us is indispensable to the health of this excessive being who is the pharmacological being – and who is healthy *only on this condition*.

In terms of the vocabulary proposed here, this means that the *pharmakon*, failing to serve the therapeutic knowledge that each

of the social systems cultivates, and failing to support any autonomy – neither of individuals nor of the groups that form the social
– on the contrary submits them to its heteronomy, a situation
systematically maintained and exploited by marketing and addictogenic society.

At the beginning of the nineteenth century, the disadjustment
between the social systems and the technical system (which is the
system of *pharmaka* referred to by Freud)[17] underwent an extraordinary increase owing to the fact that technics, science and industry arranged and configured a new epoch, characterized by constant
modernization, that is, by structural obsolescence. This is what
was called 'progress', and it dictated the imperative of permanent
innovation, but it will turn out that the eventual outcome of this
disadjustment – after passing through two global military wars
and the so-called Cold War – is a global economic war *imposing,
in the name of this war, adaptation,*[18] *that is, the renunciation of
the normativity and the individuation that Winnicott calls both
creativity and health.*

This process thereby engenders a *sterile pathogenesis* that is
both planetary in scale and extraordinarily violent. In this utterly
unprecedented situation, and precisely to the extent that, as
proletarianization, it leads to the liquidation of every form of
knowledge – *savoir-faire*, *savoir-vivre* and theoretical knowledge
– the pathogenesis grounded in the multitude of disapprenticeships
imposed through pharmacological short-circuits becomes massively toxic, because the pharmacological being proves incapable
of taking care of itself or its others.

15. New critique and the pharmacology of non-existent objects

It is as a *rational form of care*, maintaining reason through the
formation and training of deep attention of a specific kind, aiming
at the formation of apodictic statements, that is, submitted to
anamnesic, cumulative, non-contradictory and demonstrative
rules of transindividuation, that theory as such finds itself short-
circuited. But with it, and behind it, this regression affects *every
long* transindividuation circuit, not all of which are theoretical.

The theoretical is a modality of the experience of consistences, that is, of motives that form into thinking for oneself, configuring, as anamnesic necessity, a 'true self', and as such constituting thought as creativity (in Winnicott's sense).

Theoretical objects are transitional: they belong neither to the interior nor the exterior.[19] Hence the geometric point is not within the exterior: it constitutes the exterior as space, but it is not in the exterior since it has neither volume nor surface. For all that, no more is it in the interior: it is not a 'subjective' or 'psychic' reality (as Husserl demonstrated so well in *Logical Investigations*). Such objects, although they do not ex-sist (and Winnicott teaches us that this is the case for all transitional objects), nevertheless consist.

Philosophy has always believed that these objects must be understood to be transcendental, that is, rational objects par excellence. It is no longer possible to qualify them in this way, however, to the extent that the transcendental remains defined *in opposition to* the empirical – given that this opposition has been challenged by a pharmacological analysis that accords noetic virtue to tertiary retention: in the pharmacology of spirit, consistence, existence and subsistence compose, and do not oppose. And it is this consistence that makes 'life worth living' *as this composition.*

The *proletarianization of the theoretical* dries up at its very source the production of long circuits within transindividuation, by bringing dissociation (that is, the destruction of dia-logical milieus, or associated milieus, by proletarianization, which separates those who are proletarianized from their milieu, and which no longer permits them to individuate themselves by co-individuating themselves) to the highest levels of human activity: those levels in which understanding is organized with reason in order to project ideas, that is, infinities.

The fundamental question for a new critique, that is, for a pharmacology founded on a general organology, is that of *passing from ontology to genealogy without losing the ideas*, which are these consistences, and which are the most precious fruits of transitional space, that is, of the *pharmakon* of which care has been taken – and with which care is taken *of* the pharmacological being *by* the pharmacological being.

In place of the ideal beings of the ontology stemming from Platonism must be substituted those infinite objects that are consistences, reconsidered in light of the Freudian, then the Winnicottian accounts of the infinite objects that produce all libidinal economy – and that are also pure motives, in the sense that Deleuze gives to this qualification. The ideal beings of ontology must be replaced by infinite motives.

Here, the question of sublimation must be investigated anew: 'Freud used the word "sublimation" to point the way to a place where cultural experience is meaningful, but perhaps he did not get so far as to tell us where in the mind cultural experience is.'[20] Revisiting the question of this 'cultural experience', that is, of that which constitutes the possibility of the noetic, the possibility of autonomy, normativity and creativity as sublimation – all of these being dimensions of what Simondon described as psychic and collective individuation – means putting it *in its place*, which is transitional space, that is, pharmacological space.

Given that what 'Freud and Klein avoided [...] was the full implication of dependence and therefore of the environmental factor',[21] Freudian thinking in relation to the question of sublimation remains insufficient. Sublimation, as condition par excellence of autonomy, is what passes *above all* through the experience of dependence that is the heteronomy of the *pharmakon*. And this was also the issue at stake in the *Symposium*.[22]

16. Knowledge as an after-effect of pharmacological shock

This structure of pharmacological *après-coup* (which always comes after pharmacological dependence, if not always too late) is what, in the second volume of *Technics and Time*, I refer to as the *doubly epokhal redoubling*[23] – which is also the theoretical formulation of the way in which *prometheia* and *epimetheia* are arranged.[24]

Through this arrangement, Promethean pharmacology enables the constitution of an Epimethean therapeutic – of an *epimeleia* founded on a *melete*, which is itself empirical and technical, which is thus always itself drawn back to its pharmacological provenance, and which, as life of the spirit, is also the pathology of this spirit, always threatened by self-rationalization, as shown in different ways by Weber and Foucault.

The first redoubling is the primary effect by which a new *pharmakon*, causing an 'infidelity of the milieu', opens an *epokhe*, that is, a suspension of the programmes governing an epoch[25] (the three organological levels arrange psychosomatic, technical and socio-ethnic programmes, and programmatology[26] studies the specific rhythms, temporalities and spatialities these generate as cardinalities and calendarities techno-logically formed in relation to cosmic programmes and physiological programmes).[27]

This *primary suspension* short-circuits the suspended programmes, and it is pathological above all in this sense: a lesion, a wound and a weakness.

The second redoubling, the *epokhe* that constitutes an epoch properly speaking, intervenes as a therapeutic, a technics of self and others, a normativity established through a process of adoption,[28] a new form of affection. And it too is pathological but in another sense: in the sense that it forms itself against those models of adaptation – that is, of disindividuation – that the first redoubling aims to impose.

This *secondary suspension* thus invents a new *pathos* – another kind of *philia* that is also a 'form of life' – by creating new long circuits from out of the initial pharmacological shock. The transindividuation that then reconstitutes itself consists in a proteiform creative and sublimatory activity.

It is in this way that the pharmacological pathogenesis of existences (of individuals) occurs, between subsistences and consistences.

A society that does not know how to form this second moment will be destroyed – in general through absorption and integration into another society, itself constituted and reconstituted through the normative and therapeutic invention proper to a new *pharmakon*. It is thus that civilizations form and disappear – civilizations that are as such and above all mortal.

As for 'us', if we are indeed right to speak of an everyday apocalyptic feeling, the point is not merely that we risk being absorbed into another civilization: it is that there is no longer any civilization capable of absorbing 'us' – even if the vitality of Asia constitutes in this regard and according to all evidence a totally unprecedented question, *and perhaps a chance*, which means that pharmacological discussion must develop further and displace therapeutic as well as pharmacological knowledge into directions that are utterly original.

3

Pharmacology of Nuclear Fire, Generalized Automation and Total Proletarianization

17. The *pharmakon* as *automaton*

Knowledge is always constituted in a pharmacological *après-coup*, and *as* this *après-coup*:[1] it constitutes a *deferred time* of the *pharmakon* and opens the play *of its différance*.[2]

Nevertheless, industrial pharmacology, through digital syntheses of understanding that enable comprehension functions to be delegated to machines and devices, develops technologies related to what in the 1960s began to be called 'real time', installing the pharmacology of *light-time*.[3] It is in this context that the question appears of what Derrida ventured to call the 'absolute *pharmakon*': that of the atomic era, that is, of an age structurally turned toward the possibility of its nuclear auto-apocalypse.

With the military infrastructure devoted to the unleashing of nuclear fire, constituted by missile pads, output terminals of digital computer networks for which the inputs are the radars and other strategic surveillance apparatus guided by calculation systems synthesizing the functions of understanding – themselves connected to a network of networks the architecture of which lies at the origin of the Internet – the question arises of a *pharmakon* become *pure automaton*.

Moreover, the *industrial* pharmacological age is *essentially* that of automation. This begins with Jacques de Vaucanson and spreads progressively as the proletarianization of the various strata that form circuits of transindividuation. A threshold was clearly crossed with the advent of nuclear weapons, eventually resulting in the *structural* proletarianization of the politico-military commander-in-chief himself and, with him, of the sphere of politics as such – eventually resulting in the liquidation of the political body and of the regime of psychic and collective individuation specific to it, through the destruction of political knowledge,[4] to which the telecratic becoming of democracy also leads.

Paul Virilio introduced this question in *Speed and Politics* by showing how the 1962 Cuban crisis and, ten years later, the negotiations between Nixon and Brezhnev that officially aimed, if not for denuclearization, at least at limiting nuclear weapons, had as their genuine stake the preservation of the possibility of human decision, and of avoiding the total automation (that is, total proletarianization) of military pharmacological systems.[5]

Beginning with the simulation systems for the radar/missile systems of both East and West, however, these technologies that were military in origin rapidly migrated towards management, then towards markets and the most everyday social practices, as real-time interactive systems, firstly in the spheres of the stock market, entertainment and banking, eventually becoming practically ubiquitous. This was especially so with the development of digital networks beginning with the Arpanet, which became the Internet, weaving the fabric that is the World Wide Web, a new pharmacological milieu if ever there was one, and as a result of which carbon-time gave way to light-time.

This is why what Cornell University called 'nuclear criticism', referring to a colloquium in which Jacques Derrida participated in April 1984, carried to its apocalyptic extremes, and as a pharmacology of nuclear fire, a much more general question of the *pharmakon* of which the stake is speed:

> Are we having today *another* experience of speed? Is our relation to time and to motion becoming qualitatively different? Or, on the contrary, can we not speak of an extraordinary, although qualitatively homogeneous, acceleration of the same experience? And on what temporality are we relying when we put the question that way? It goes without saying that we can't take the question seriously without reelaborating all the problematics of time and

motion, from Aristotle to Heidegger by way of Augustine, Kant, Husserl, Einstein, and Bergson.[6]

18. The spatialized time of the *pharmakon* and the step beyond

If it is true, however, that the thinking of work and its relation to capital essentially passes, since Marx, through the question of time and its measurement, then without convoking Marxist philosophy here, in this meditation on the questions opened by the nuclear age and by the hypotheses of nuclear criticism, does this not lead to a major geopolitical and economico-political choice – and a choice very prejudicial to the crossing of a necessary *step beyond*?

For, ultimately, the 'absolute *pharmakon*' that provokes these questions extends to the *totality* of social relations the Marxist question of the *measurement of time by its technical spatialization* (through what I describe as tertiarization, which is a grammatization). Daniel Bensaïd, for example, repeats Augustine's question – 'If it is by time that we measure the movement of bodies, how can we measure time itself?'[7] – thereby recalling that capitalism solves this question *factually*, through the technical *abstraction of labour time*, an abstraction lying within the principles of capitalism as the short-circuit of the time of noetic souls,[8] that is, the short-circuit *of the right and duty of individuation*, and of what Canguilhem or Winnicott named creativity or normativity:

> In order that such measurement could become conceivable, we had to suspend that which ceaselessly 'transforms and diversifies itself', standardize the diversity of movement, spatialize duration [...], capital reducing the particular time of *savoir-faire* [...] to abstract social time.[9]

This time of *savoir-faire* is that of desire, even for the most minor work activity *insofar as it is not reducible to employment*, that is, insofar as a *savoir-faire* is creatively cultivated through it (this is precisely what constitutes *savoir-faire*), and as contribution to the individuation of a world constituting an associated milieu. Proletarianization, on the other hand, consists precisely in a process of dissociation,[10] that is, of social sterilization.

It is thus desire and its proteiform transformations, which is also to say, *all forms of will*, that find themselves short-circuited by the technologies of temporal measurement that characterize the industrial age of the *pharmakon*. These short-circuits now thoroughly traverse society:

> the nuclear age *gives us to think* this aporia of speed starting from the limit of absolute acceleration, such that in the uniqueness of an ultimate event, of a final collision or collusion, the temporalities called subjective and objective, phenomenological and intra-worldly, authentic and inauthentic, originary or 'vulgar', would end up being merged into one another – playing here with Bergsonian, Husserlian and Heideggerian categories.[11]

Here there is no longer any reference to Aristotle or Einstein, and we can well understand why not. But nor is there any reference to Marxist categories, and this is far less comprehensible.

19. *Les coups*. Living pharmacologically

The rich developments that emerged from this conference, published under the title 'No Apocalypse, Not Now', come to the following conclusion: a *critique* of the nuclear age *is not possible*. If nuclear criticism is necessary, as are new forms of study developed thereafter in the United States, what would nevertheless make this new paradigm seem problematic is the fact that the very category of 'critique' is now outdated.

According to Derrida, ' "Nuclear criticism", like Kantian criticism, is a thinking about the limits of experience as a thinking of finitude', and, for this Kantian criticism, 'the history of humanity [is the] example of finite rationality', that is, of *intuitus derivativus* in relation to the *intuitus originarius* of a divine and *infinite* intellect,[12] and thus 'presupposes the possibility of an *infinite* progress regulated on an idea of reason'.[13] Given all this, nuclear criticism 'would make it possible to think the very limit of criticism':

> This limit comes into view in the groundlessness of a remainderless self-destruction of the self, auto-destruction of the *autos* itself. Whereupon is shattered the nucleus of criticism itself.[14]

But what would enable an advance on such an affirmation? What is it about the *factual* possibility of 'the self-destruction of the very *"autos"*'' that makes it *necessary*, that is, *right [en droit]*, to shatter 'the very nucleus of criticism'?

Without doubt it is the fact that this *autos*, which only claims to constitute itself *in law [en droit]* by positing its *absolute autonomy* as a principle, is *in fact* never *constituted* other than through the accidentality of a *pharmakon* that is absolutely empirical, that is, heteronomic – 'autonomy' always having its *provenance* (and this would be a fact that could never be *opposed* to a right) in a primary heteronomy, autonomy being therefore always *relative*. This relative autonomy is a *relational* autonomy, and relational autonomy (which is also to say, dialogical autonomy)[15] *composes* with heteronomy; it plays creatively with transitional space, as one could also say. It invents norms in the enormity of pharmacological pathogenesis, like that child that is time.[16]

But if it can be granted that the primary *epokhe* that can cause any *pharmakon* to short-circuit *may also* constitute itself *après-coup* as a system of care, reconstituting long circuits grounded in anamneses, that is, in creative and normative individuation processes providing the feeling that life is *worth* living, that life is *worth the BLOW, the COUP,* of being lived (which is something that can never be proven) – for example, as the noetic activity of a *krinein* that might very well have denied its pharmacological provenance throughout its 'metaphysical' history, and as such denied its grammatological constitution, but which in spite of all that was not made in vain – then it remains unclear why 'the very nucleus of criticism' would be condemned to 'shatter'.

Rather, it is *necessary to care for oneself*, to *learn to live* pharmaco-logically, that is, normatively, affected and even *wounded* as one may be by the infidelity of pharmacology – of the pharmacology of Spirit, which comes to blows [*heurte de ses coups*] with the spirits of Valéry, Husserl, Freud, Benjamin, Adorno, Horkheimer, Habermas, Anders and so many others – through which its original pathogenetic content is revealed.

'Caring for oneself' here means not renouncing reason, motives for living, that which makes life worth the blow and the pain of being lived. This means: not renouncing the noetic that *transitionally infinitizes* its objects, which is what Valéry called Spirit; and yet not ignoring all kinds of sublimation processes that have a phantasmatic essence that can never be isolated, thus which are, in other words, an imaginative activity coming from the unconscious and from *its* critique (in both senses of the genitive), that is, from transitional practices through which it is projected towards the real and via the symbolic, practices that can always be inverted and become their opposite and thus, like fire, become that which, as the origin of civilization, also constitutes the possibility of its negation and its end – the possibility of apocalypse, that is, of what must and can *remain impossible*.

20. Wanting to deconstruct

The nucleus that, according to Derrida, nuclear criticism would shatter, is the 'transcendental subject' that constitutes the three syntheses of imagination, and the schematism that they prop up, through which the categories of understanding are constituted – the transcendental imagination that, according to Kant, precedes images, that is, precedes the *pharmaka* that always threaten to proletarianize understanding: to draw the subject back to its minority. It was to counter this threat that the Enlightenment wanted to *conquer* majority *for all*.

Now, *what* does deconstruction *want*, if not to constitute an *ultra-maturity* [*super-majorité*] for deconstructors, who would thus no longer be taken in by and no longer themselves repeat the lures of pure autonomy? What could it mean to claim that the nucleus has been 'shattered', if not that one will *no longer* be taken in by the blinding effects of the *pharmakon*?

But does such a claim not amount to hyper-criticism? To ask this question is to enter into and to claim to have undertaken a hyper-critique of the limits of deconstruction (this is what I have outlined in 'Fidelity at the Limits of Deconstruction').[17] It is to ask if such a programme is pharmacologically sustainable – if it has not always already pharmacologically shattered, while not ceasing to redouble itself in the *après-coup of that which is worthwhile* [*vaut*], that is, of that which is *necessary* [*faut*]: the default.

Is it possible to reduce the pharmaco-logy of the *pharmaka*? Evidently not. Nobody has said better than Derrida why this is so. It is necessary to *make do*, or to *make the most of things* – that is, to make do with or make the most of the fact that *life is in the end ONLY worth living pharmacologically*, and in particular as deconstruction of the logic of the *pharmakon*, as deluded [*leurrée*] as such an operation can *itself* remain at its 'nucleus', if it is necessary to have an originary point of *absolute singularity* around which such a nucleus is formed.[18]

For in any case the deconstructor – who regularly claims the gesture of the *Aufklärer* in spite of everything that Derrida asserts *à propos* criticism and critique[19] – would be unable to reduce the pharmacological condition that he deconstructs, which means that he himself projects lures and casts delusions that he is not himself able to see. These delusions are not necessarily those of a promised or conquered autonomy: they can clearly be 'negative', and in some way hyper-limiting or hyper-inhibitors – nightmares, apocalyptic discourses of all kinds, various attacks of acute melancholy, chained to or stuck in absolute heteronomy, the liver exposed.

Such is the insurmountable lot of pharmacological beings.

21.   The discernment of the lovable

What permits *both* the nucleus and its delusions, including those that are 'negative', that is, self-destructive, what permits this point of singularity at the origin of all deconstruction as its self-decomposition in the face of the heterogeneous, is the libidinal economy of an infinite desire for an infinite singularity on the part of a singularity itself infinite, that is, always incomplete, but often fatigued by its never finishing, that is, always susceptible to regression.

This infinity, which distinguishes justice from the law and the promise from the programme – and this is what leads Derrida to regularly venture the term 'quasi-transcendental' – no longer presents itself to us as a Kantian question, but rather as a Freudian question. It is the novelty of this difference that opens the site for a new critique.

The consideration of this infinity cannot, however, be contained within Freudian thought alone: it must pass through Winnicott and through the transitional object, that is, the *pharmakon*. We shall return to this in the following chapter.

Derrida claims that the nucleus of criticism shatters because it equates critical possibility with absolute autonomy, thereby excluding the possibility of a relational criticism. The necessity of initially posing such an equivalence is completely understandable: such is the way that philosophical critique has always been thought, from the Platonic question '*ti esti?*' to the Kantian questions ('What can I know?', 'What must I do?', 'What can I hope for?', 'What is human?'), and beyond. Such a claim (that 'the very nucleus of criticism shatters' because critical possibility is *equivalent* to absolute autonomy) presupposes that criticism and critique are conceivable *only* as noetic acts of a *purely* autonomous subject.

Derrida opposes to this autonomy an automatism of the *pharmakon*. Deconstruction is itself, in effect, a kind of automatic process, beginning by way of a primary suspension, an *epokhal* redoubling:

> Deconstruction takes place, it is an event that does not await the deliberation, consciousness, or organization of a subject, or even of modernity. It deconstructs itself. [...] And the 'se' [the self] of 'se deconstruire' [deconstructs itself], which is not the reflexivity of an ego or of a consciousness, bears the whole enigma.[20]

What is this *automatic reflexivity* outside the self or the ego, without ego, before all ego, if not the *becoming industrial of transitional space*, and the institution, as grammatization, of a *rapidity* that ends up bypassing or short-circuiting the psychosomatic work of transindividuation, *that is, that leads to the proletarianizing of everything that thinks and moves?* This automatic reflexivity, this reflexive system, is also Freud's 'perfecting of organs' – and the *primary* movement of that *pharmakon* that is always already deconstructing the pathogenetic being. This 'spontaneous' deconstruction – which, when confronted with the Derridian 'quasi-transcendental', it would be tempting to call (wrongly) 'quasi-natural' – accelerates in the industrial age of the *pharmakon* and seems to liquidate the very transitional character of pharmacological space that has been systemically proletarianized.

Neither grammatology nor deconstruction is sufficient to *treat* [*soigner*] this: it requires an organology, that is, a history of the supplement yet to see the light of day, deconstruction having always remained encamped in the undecidable logic of the supplement – as if the *automaton* alone can discriminate or, as Deleuze says, 'bifurcate', if not critique, and can only do so through the tremors of its automatic crises.

Now, there is a second moment in this automatic reflexivity. It is not a re-appropriation, which would be a return to the proper, that is, a purification of the *pharmakon*, the elimination of its poisonous side. It is, rather, the moment of *adoption*, which is utterly to the contrary of adaptation, the latter being precisely an automatic submission to the *automaton*.

Adoption, which is a process of individuation, the *différance* of a *doing* [*faire avec*: doing, or making the most of, or making do with] *what is worthwhile*, is hyper-pharmaco-logical, and constitutes what Derrida called '*exappropriation*': an appropriation always on the way towards the dis-appropriation of its *alteration*, to the extent that *its object is that of its desire*, that is, of its unconscious, and not only of its consciousness. But such an adoption, as a struggle against proletarianization – thus as 'deproletarianization' – necessitates a politics: it is a question not only of psychotherapy but of sociotherapy.

Transitional adoption, which is thoroughly pharmacological, constitutes the re-arming of a relational critical faculty, above all as discernment of the lovable – and as the *epimetheia* of contemporary *prometheia*. It is an experience of desire, that is, of a 'proper' and a self or ego that always already projects *itself* outside itself, beyond the self and into that which is never absolutely one's own because it is, precisely, one's other.

But such a projection is *also* a reflexivity: a pharmacological and phantasmatic mirror that no longer claims pure autonomy, but which, insofar as it treats and takes care of [*soigné*] itself, and through this takes care of transitional space, always affirms the absolute infinitude of its object: its consistence – its promise.

22.   The displacement of the infinite

This is the question of the infinite and its interminable *displacement*. The infinite constitutes the horizon of the critical subject, the nucleus of criticism. Rationalization, in the sense given to this term by Adorno and Horkheimer and by Weber, is the finitization of the world, and proletarianization is the death of God, that is, of *that* infinity that constitutes the horizon of Kantian criticism – as that which projects itself as motive of reason (idea) become *progress to the infinite* for that finite being endowed with an *intuitus derivativus*:

> The *intuitus derivativus* of the receptive (that is, perceiving) being, of which the human subject is only one example, cuts its figure out on the (back)ground of the possibility of an *intuitus originarius*, of an infinite intellect that creates rather than invents its own objects.[21]

Now, Husserl displaces the question of the finite, of the infinite, of their play and their opposition, by breaking with Kant on precisely this point:

> God, the Subject of absolutely perfect knowledge, and therefore also of every possible adequate perception, naturally possesses what is denied to finite beings such as ourselves: the perception of things in themselves. But this view is nonsensical. It implies that there is no *essential difference* between transcendent and immanent, that in the postulated divine intuition a spatial thing is a real [*reelles*] constituent, and indeed a lived experience itself, a constituent of the stream of the divine consciousness and the divine lived experience.[22]

In the Husserlian eidetic, this opposition between the finite and the infinite is 'nonsensical'. The *eidos* of red, '*the*' red, *which does not exist*, is the condition of possibility of any experience of red; it is what is *aimed at* in all red experiences, experiences of such and such red, and this inexistence is an infinitude of red that opens the indeterminate possibility of all finite reds. The Husserlian transcendental subject can *intuitively know* (something forbidden in Kant by the separation of understanding and intuition), which means that it is a projector of infinite objects for practices themselves infinite – for example, painting or geometry. This is why geometry opens the community of a *we*, itself infinite: the *we* of geometry forms a circuit of transindividuation that is in principle [*en droit*] infinite, and geometry *is* this principle [*droit*].

Derrida called this transitional dimension of phenomenology 'spectral' (and 'hauntological'):[23]

> [T]he radical possibility of all spectrality should be sought in the direction that Husserl identifies, in such a surprising but forceful way, as an intentional but *non-real* [*non-réelle*] component of the phenomenological lived experience, namely the *noeme*. Unlike the three other terms of the two correlations (*noese-noeme*, *morphe-hule*), this non-reality [*non-réellité*], this intentional but *non-real* inclusion of the noematic correlate is neither 'in' the world nor 'in' consciousness. But it is precisely the condition of any experience, any objectivity, any phenomenality, namely of any noetico-noematic correlation [...]. Is it not [...] what inscribes the possibility of the other and of mourning right onto the phenomenality of the phenomenon?[24]

As strange as it may seem at first sight, this is also, primordially, the infant's experience of transitional objects and transitional phenomena. Such experiences 'belong to the realm of illusion which is at the basis of initiation of experience':

> This intermediate area of experience, unchallenged in respect of its belonging to inner or external (shared) reality, constitutes the greater part of the infant's experience, and throughout life is retained in the intense experiencing that belongs to the arts and to religion and to imaginative living, and to creative scientific work.[25]

In other words, the intuitive experience of infinite objects of knowledge, that is, of consistences, is opened up by that projector of infinities that is the unconscious – and reason is as such above all a matter of desire. In the course of this experience an economy is constituted which is that of *investment in the object*, through which the object can appear, that is, be aimed at and intentionalized:

> In object-relating the subject allows certain alterations in the self to take place, of a kind that has caused us to invent the term cathexis [that is, investment]. The object has become meaningful. Projection mechanisms and identifications have been operating.[26]

To which Winnicott adds this question: '[I]f play is neither inside nor outside, where is it?'[27]

The hauntological and spectral structure of phenomenology as analysed by Derrida, or in other words the structure of intentionality, presupposes a transitional space where the real, redoubled through and in the encounter with the *pharmakon* (for example, for the proto-geometer, first of all as surveying), redoubles itself symbolically, and as the infinitude of the imaginary.

This is possible only insofar as a therapeutic is implemented, making the unconscious speak and *consist* (the unconscious being a condition of what Husserl called the faculty of reactivation, 'that belongs originally to every human being as a speaking being',[28] and that itself presupposes the capacity for anamnesis), and thus, whether it does or does not pass through consciousness, it invents another epoch of decision, *krisis*, that is, of discernment or judgement, *krinon*, of *analusis*, decomposition, and so on: all categories without which there can be no critique, and which are themselves only known by passing through critique.

There is, then, in fact and in principle, a double critique:

- that which operates the *pharmakon* 'behind consciousness', unconsciously – that is, outside consciousness, but not yet through *the* unconscious, which is a psychic agency, and not merely a pharmacological one;
- that which operates consciousness from new motives coming from the unconscious, because they have been *made projectable and schematizable* by the redoubling of the critique induced by the first moment of the *pharmakon*.

This second moment is the one that, concerning the *pharmakon* of the letter, I have described in *Technics and Time, 2* as a process of *différantial* identification induced by the literalization of utterances and the new relation to the context of utterance as well as reading in which it results.[29] For in fact, the unconscious is dialogical, and as such related to what Julia Kristeva, reader of Bakhtin, calls intertextuality.[30] But intertexuality is only a particular case within the pharmacology of the unconscious. And here it would clearly be necessary to evoke Simondon's concept of the 'preindividual milieu' in order to make these statements more precise.

23. Deproletarianization

The process of grammatization – an expression that extends and alters a concept taken from Sylvain Auroux – is the history of the supplement that consists in a *discretization*, a *discrimination*, an *analysis* and a *decomposition* of flux or flows, *critical* operations of the *pharmakon* that, as the first moment [*coup*] of the primary suspension, traverse pharmacological being. This includes: operations performed on speech (such as 'written expression' and 'written signs'); but also on bodily gestures (the machine tool and everything that leads to the automation of the production apparatus, speech being also a production of the body, but where the denial of its pharmacological constitution led to the opposition of body and soul, with the result that the corporeality of speech became unthinkable); and then on light and sound frequencies that stimulate the senses (analogue technologies); and finally operations of understanding (digital technologies).

What opens the Derridian problematic in Husserl is, strictly speaking, the thought of the hypomnesic genesis of geometric anamnesis, the latter becoming the reactivation of the 'originary intuitions' of the proto-geometer. Although he thus shows that the *pharmakon* of writing, and thus hypomnesis, is the condition of *anamnesis*, that is, of the critique of the *pharmakon* and its epokhal redoubling, Derrida *himself* never sought the possibility of a second moment, that is, of a secondary suspension which, as *après-coup*, constitutes new circuits of transindividuation from out of the short-circuits provoked by proletarianization. Why not?

There are many reasons. I shall only examine two.

The first reason is that industrial pharmacology constitutes a completely new configuration for which the possibility of secondary redoubling can be thought only as the object of an economico-political struggle in regard to the relation to instruments of *negotium*, and such that it can become the vector of a new libidinal economy, of unprecedented processes of sublimation, and of the invention of a new age of *otium* – an *otium* of the people.

Certainly, Derrida, like many others, and in the first place Benjamin, strives to think the possibility of a redoubling of the apparatuses (that is, of the industrial *pharmaka*) of artistic practice, as can be seen for example in those statements through which the art of photography is considered with and from the photo-graphic apparatus itself.[31] But ultimately Derrida never offered any thematic treatment of such apparatus in terms of its being an element within a process of the grammatization of perception, a process fundamentally tied to the discretization of corporal flows and thus to proletarianization, and he therefore never envisaged the possible proletarianization of art *as* the possibility of such an *après-coup*.

The process of grammatization as source of proletarianization is inscribed within a geopolitical and economic history, a history within which the powers that take control of it (and first of all as the power of the Church over minds in the age of colonization, and through its missions, but also through the Reformation,[32] then biopower and, finally, psychopower)[33] attempted, from the moment that grammatization of the body made possible capitalist organization and rationalization (in the Weberian sense and that of Adorno and Horkheimer), to promote the belief that the loss of individuation characteristic of each new pharmacological stage is *inevitable* and *incurable*.

Confronted with such a situation, it is not enough to decon-struct metaphysics: it is necessary to fight against this ideology and to engage a new critique of political economy. For, by exploit-ing the short-circuits caused by the primary suspension in which a *pharmakon* always above all consists, these powers were able to draw profits from them, profits that, in the context of an eco-nomic war become global, are in part reinvested in permanent innovation, that is, in the constant production of new types of *pharmaka* according to an ever more sustained rhythm inducing a 'torpor of [the worker's] mind', as Adam Smith put it.[34] And this torpor does not only affect the minds of workers become proletarian, however, but also the minds of clerics – become 'intellectuals'.

This is why the new critique – which is always historically situ-ated (that is, pharmacologically situated), and which revolves, first and foremost, around the specific traits of the *industrial pharma-kon* inasmuch as its genesis proceeds essentially, functionally and programmatically from the economic sphere (from *negotium*) – must above all be dedicated to analysing processes of expropria-tion insofar as they aim to restrict *différance to the shortest possible circuits in order to gain the most rapid possible return on investment.*

This rapidity, which is not that of the *pharmakon*, but which is made possible by the industrial *pharmakon*, leads to a pharmacology of capital[35] in which investment is *annihilated* by speculation, the chronic obsolescence of objects destroying psychic transitional investments as much as the economic structures of production. From that point, desire – as the binding of the drives, which are trans-formed through this binding (beyond the pleasure principle and what Derrida called the 'PR/PP stricture')[36] into libidinal energy (which maintains and contains the drives just as Hestia maintains and contains the fire of the hearth) – finds itself unbound and decomposed. The 'spirit of capitalism' thereby reveals itself to be the pharmacology most poisonous for the spirit, in which there proliferates apocalyptic discourse, feelings and tones of all kinds, and as banality itself.

Proletarianization is a fact in the face of which de-proletarianization is not only a right but a duty. It is a right and a duty for the psychic economy as much as for the economy of subsistence. An economy that is no longer capable of fostering the feeling that life is worth living, and that *essentially* provokes the loss of the feeling of existing, is condemned to collapse. And this loss of the feeling of existing, which was expressed in these very terms by Richard Durn shortly before he embarked on a massacre that turned him into a celebrity, and who promptly thereafter committed suicide,[37] was also described by Winnicott in order to introduce the question of the drives: 'The instincts [the drives] are the main threat to play as to the ego; in seduction some external agency exploits the child's instincts and helps to annihilate the child's sense of existing as an autonomous unit, making play impossible.'[38]

In the epoch of psychopower, the exploitation of the first pharmacological redoubling emerging from the industrial grammatization of attention is what, by short-circuiting transindividuation, tends to seduce and exploit the drives of the psychic apparatus, which are thereby deprived of existence, that is, of singularity, because the latter resists that hyper-synchronization of production behaviour, consumption behaviour *and conception behaviour* (like the '*pensée unique*' found in economics, science and the political sphere[39]) that presupposes the industrial production of the mass. By this very fact, this exploitation (which *is* proletarianization) tends to cancel out any possibility of a second suspension, that is, of an Epimethean *praxis* of the *prometheia* constituted by the new pharmacological space. Only such a *praxis*, however, enables the formation of new therapeutic forms.

Taking care of this praxical and praxiological possibility constituted in a theoretical mode is a task that the noetic has always been charged[40] with the burden of undertaking – and, in particular, philosophy. Such a 'charge' has always been a fight against that which, in transitional space, harbours regressive tendencies, whether political or economic, which is also to say, a fight against that which, in the psychic apparatus, tends towards regression. Such a fight can only be conducted in relation to the existing historical and pharmacological context, and today, in the face of industrial *organization*, this demands organological analyses grounded in a conceptual apparatus capable of identifying the original systemic dynamics that form between the three levels of general organology.[41]

Proletarianization is in a very general way and across the most diverse paths a capturing of attentional fluxes by the tertiary retentions that *pharmaka* constitute:[42] it is a destruction of attentional models that already in 1776 was being described by Adam Smith, and it is precisely what Simone Weil described in 1934 in 'Experience of Factory Life', even if she did not thematize it in this form. But it is also what happens to the consumer as the capturing, diverting and distracting of attention, a distraction in Adorno's sense (the roots of which lie in Pascal), and it is equally what occurs with the loss of attention that in politics results in the impossibility of making decisions, leading to resignation and to the exploitation of the drives incited through industrial populism – via which a state of chronic carelessness and negligence is established, paving the way for extremely acute socio-political crises. It is, finally, what proletarianizes theory such that attention is no longer paid to consistences.

I have tried to show that this was already the issue in Socrates' remarks to Hippocrates in *Protagoras*,[43] and it was also clearly in play in Simone Weil's description of the months she spent at the Alsthom factory, after her encounter with Boris Souvarine:

The fact that one is not at home in the factory, that one does not have the rights of the city, that one is a stranger accepted as a mere intermediary between machines and what they produce, this fact affects the body and the soul; under this suffering, the flesh and thought withdraw.[44]

Thought withdraws. This turning in upon the present produces a kind of stupor. The only future that one can bear to think about, beyond which thought lacks the strength to go, is that instant when one finishes the piece on which one is currently working, if the worker is lucky enough to grab such a moment.[45]

This withdrawal of thought and of the body, which is made possible because the *savoir-faire* of the worker has passed into the machines before which these workers henceforth find themselves proletarians, also in the most general way deprives consumers of their *savoir-vivre*, forcing them to constantly try to keep up with the obsolescence of things. This is so because the milieu has become fundamentally unfaithful, but according to a rhythm that no longer permits the production of new forms of fidelity, or of *pathos* producer of *philia*, or of trust, and it is the result of a much larger process that, as 'absolute *pharmakon*', thereby deprives political leaders of the very possibility of making decisions and deprives scientists of the capacity to theorize their practice, that is, to form long circuits.

And yet, *this process is not in any way the ontological law of a techno-logical second nature*: it is a situation that arises from the *carelessness of thought itself* before an *automaton* the deployment of which is confused with the fatality of an *automatic becoming* [*devenir automatique*], that is, a becoming without future [*sans avenir*].

This process sets the *pharmacological scene for a relation of forces between spirit and itself*, between two of its aspects, *otium* and *negotium* – such that they henceforth appear to constitute the tendencies of a libidinal economy that alone makes possible practices of care, beginning with those that the love of a mother for her child teaches it to bring into play, as a *learning to live* that tends in our time to be ruined by *processes of disapprenticeship* that begin earlier and earlier and at the very heart of this relation of care, and it is as a struggle against this, and against everything that comes along to solicit and seduce the drives, that the mother forms the primordial knowledge without which the infantile psychic apparatus cannot manage to constitute itself normatively.

A *second reason* that Derrida did not thematize the question of the second moment [*coup*], even though he was essentially a thinker of the *après-coup*, is that an obstacle to taking up this question of the capturing of attention as control of intentionality (attention being itself always a construction through a therapeutic, precisely from the inversion of the pharmacological default into that which is necessary)[46] lies in the fact that Derrida, in *Speech and Phenomena*,[47] while contesting with good reason the opposition of primary and secondary retention, ends up practically *abolishing* the *difference* between primary retention and secondary retention, rather than analysing the play of their composition, something that prevents him as well from thematizing tertiary retention.[48]

24. After intoxication – the age of the *après-coup*

That the time for the *après-coup* has come is neither a fact nor a right bestowed by philosophical decree: it is what is taking place in society today as a new relation of forces – as the new creativity and normativity that make possible a transitional space the characteristics of which in turn make possible the overcoming of the functional opposition between producers and consumers. This is what *Ars Industrialis* has been describing for the past five years, and it is what the struggle for free software is about, and more generally the philosophy of 'open source' and 'creative commons', and the numerous unprecedented practices emerging from collaborative technologies, all of which foreshadow what we call an economy of contribution.

Such struggles pose anew the questions of individual and collective investment, of property, of the proper and ex-appropriation, and of new forms of psychic and collective individuation – which is also to say, of sublimation – elaborated through these struggles. This is why *Ars Industrialis* unconditionally supports free software activists: their struggle is firstly that of engineers and technicians, subjected to the proletarianized condition that has been imposed upon them by the cybernetic division of their labour, which thereby ceases to be work and becomes merely a job[49] (that of 'developer', that is, a producer of code – within the process of digital grammatization, and as its first moment).

Through their struggles, from out of which an individuation is reconstituted, that is, a *self*, these 'workers of the spirit' are engaged in the age of de-proletarianization – which is a kind of disintoxication.

Today we all know that non-inhuman-kind in its totality, composed of pharmacological beings, that is, potentially inhuman beings, must disintoxicate itself. Consider: the struggle to ban smoking in enclosed public places (and where the sale of cigarettes was methodically promoted by marketing on the basis of the analyses of Bernays, himself inspired by his uncle Sigmund Freud); the removal of asbestos from buildings, a material that until recently was systematically used in construction; the establishment of new regimes of healthy eating, in order to struggle against that pathology that has become so prominent in industrialized countries, that is, obesity; as well as in a thousand other areas, and above all the consumption and production of energy, the methods of agricultural production, the size of the carbon footprint involved in the transportation of goods, and so on. In all these cases attempts are being made to find new models capable of freeing people from the poisonous explosion of *pharmaka*.

But the true question is the colossal attentional disequilibrium affecting infantile psychic systems, and the technological and pharmacological stupidity produced by systems for capturing psychopower and by the situation of generalized proletarianization, which spreads and generalizes a state of systemic stupidity that becomes the law of drive-based capitalism and industrial populism.

This *irreducibly* pharmacological being will *never* be rid of the threat that is constituted by every *pharmakon*, and that is symbolized by fire as both technics and desire. This is why the condition of all forms of possible disintoxication is the establishment of a new relation to *pharmaka* as the *après-coup of intoxication* and the *process of spreading disintoxication*, aiming no longer at a transcendental nucleus of criticism, but at the *everyday or ordinary capacity for discernment of the extra-ordinary* that supports the individuation of those who, each ensconced within the mystery of their skill or their craft, their *métier*, and of its ministry (including those of the mother and her child), have creative and normative access to transitional space, and who thus learn – for themselves and for others – why and how life is worth living.

Part II

Pharmacology of Nihilism

4

The Thing, *Kenosis* and the Power to Infinitize

But he emptied himself.

Paul of Tarsus

25. Nihilism and grammatization

Every society, whatever its form, is *above all* an apparatus for the production of fidelity.

We have learned from Max Weber that capitalism transformed the type of fidelity that had structured Western society, changing it from a society grounded in the faith of monotheistic religious belief to a society based on trust understood as fiduciary calculability. The crisis of capitalism that was unleashed in 2007, however, a crisis the extent of which was not revealed until 2008, has taught us that this transformation of fidelity into calculability, effected through the financial apparatus, has now encountered a limit whereby credit has undergone a massive inversion, turning into what I have tried to think for a number of years as 'discredit', and as a completely new form of dis-belief or miscreance [*mécréance*]. The subprime mortgage crisis and the fraud perpetrated by Bernie Madoff are both symptoms of this situation.

This becoming, which is related to what both Weber and Adorno referred to as the disenchantment brought about by rationalization, is essentially linked to a process of grammatization. This process took on a new dimension during the Renaissance with the invention of the printing press, becoming with the Reformation a site of unprecedented politico-religious struggle. In the course of these struggles, the pharmacology of the spirit constituted by the Book, and by books, and the therapeutic that such *pharmaka* require, became the centre of a spiritual conflict underpinning a new religious and secular therapeutic.

Although the Western pharmacology of spirit is certainly not reducible to its relationship with the Book and with books, it is nevertheless clearly shaped by the relation to these bookish *pharmaka*. And given that pharmacology in general is not limited to what affects the mind or spirit, it is therefore not reducible to the objects emerging from processes of grammatization, processes that, through industrialization, affect bodies in general, including their movements, perception, and the higher functions of the central nervous system. Furthermore, these grammatization processes now also affect social relations as such, as well as the very structure of life itself and the hypermaterial structure found on the quantum scale, in the end integrating *all* objects, which are linked together within an 'internet of things'.[1]

The printing press, as the main factor in what Sylvain Auroux calls the second technological revolution of grammatization, plays a decisive role in the linkage that, at the end of the Reformation and the beginning of capitalism, takes place between, on the one hand, grammatization and the pharmacology of spirit, and, on the other hand, grammatization and the pharmacology of bodies. The printing press constitutes a mutation in the meaning of literal grammatization: a 'pharmacological turn' is produced, which, however, precedes the grammatization of gesture constitutive of the mechanical age, and which consists in the submission of *hypomnemata* to the imperatives of *accounting*, that is, of *negotium*. This transformation remains largely unthought, even though the turn will have been the object of that major spiritual struggle that was the Reformation as a therapeutic of reading, and that was a temporal struggle as the implementation of an instrumentalization of accounting.

Within this turn, it is the relationship between *otium* and *negotium* that changes: this becoming passes through a new socialization of *hypomnemata*, eventually resulting, as the use of account books spreads and becomes commonplace (a possibility deriving from the massive reading practice in which the Reformation essentially consists), in the formation of *ratio* understood not only as reason but as calculation – and does so well before Descartes, in whom Heidegger sees the determining factor, whereas the Cartesian event was actually an after-effect, and something like a therapeutic proposition.

Divine *logos* becomes secular *ratio*: this fact lies at the foundation of America, and it is well known that in this regard Weber draws attention to the historical meaning of the sermon in which Benjamin Franklin pushed *pro nobis* to an extreme. This was referred to by Mark Taylor in 1984:

> The conclusion of this quest for salvation can be summed up by the theological doctrine implied in the formula *pro nobis*. What Christ means, claimed Luther, is grounded in 'the fact' that he lived and died *for us*.[2]

This becoming is translated into the inscription found on the dollar bill, which, proposing that 'In God we trust', is no longer quite the same as a statement of *belief* in God.

This odd evolution of the verb designating the relationship of fidelity of noetic creatures to their Creator would be incomprehensible were it not inscribed on paper money, which *thereby* constitutes a unit of accounting. And it is this *relation* to that which consists (and to *He* who consists) on a plane other than that of creatures, a relation constituted in a relation to the Book, that is hence affected by that which, in Nietzsche's language, takes the name of nihilism – Heidegger claiming that with this name, for Nietzsche, it is the *suprasensible in its totality that is put into question*. And we shall return to this point.

Nietzsche claimed that it would take a long time before those who murdered God would be capable of comprehending their gesture:

> I have come too early [...]. This tremendous event is still on its way, still wandering; it has not yet reached the ears of men. Lightning and thunder require time; the light of the stars requires time; deeds, though done, still require time to be seen and heard.[3]

If so, then perhaps we, some one hundred and thirty years after this pronouncement (which dates from 1884, in *The Gay Science*), have entered into the ordeal of this revelation *as such*. Today, perhaps, the black night, and not only the shadows announcing it, at last befalls us, and does so as that apocalypticism without God that presently haunts the entire world, given that since 2008 the consumerist model, by *collapsing*, has clearly shown that it is no longer only the fiduciary objects of *logos*, constituted by *hypomnemata*, which, in terms of their meaning and their social function, have changed in the course of the twentieth century, but quotidian and familiar objects as well – and with them, and as what at bottom they alone can definitively shatter, *das Ding*, the Thing.

26.   *Ding,* things and garage sales

What is this Thing? We will not here conduct the thorough reading of texts by Freud and Lacan that such a question calls for – but this will be the subject of *La Technique et le Temps 5: La guerre des esprits*. Briefly and provisionally, it can be said that the first occurrence of 'the Thing' appears very early, in the famous *Project for a Scientific Psychology*,[4] and that according to Lacan it describes the structure of desire,[5] insofar as the latter consists in a process of substitution thoroughly haunted by a lack, and where all objects of desire refer to this Thing, which would be the substitutive expression of this lack.

One could say that the Thing is the object of all desire – but this is an object *that does not exist*, if, as Lacan says, there has never been an *experience* of this Thing. As Bernard Baas has brilliantly shown, *das Ding*, which does not exist, constitutes as such a kind of a priori of desire.[6] For the moment we can say that the Thing, as object of all desires, opens (like *theos* in Aristotle) every horizon of expectation, and as such constitutes *archi-protention*.

As for things – the *Things* about which Perec writes,[7] and such that they now form (that is, since the 1960s) the 'system of objects' made famous by Jean Baudrillard[8] – they still constitute, until the beginning of the twentieth century, the shared milieu within which relations of fidelity are formed. Things tie, seal and support these relations, as objects of inheritance, work, the formation of knowledge, shared activities, games, commerce of all kinds, and so on, but also and above all as *transitional objects*: those of the *infans* as well as those of *sublimation*.

Now, these thingly supports of everyday life, which supported the world and the making-world essentially grounded in and through this making-trust, have become *disposable and structurally obsolescent* as capitalism has brought into being what Schumpeter theorized in his *Theory of Economic Evolution*, namely, the chronic obsolescence of industrial products henceforth furnished and swept away by a permanent innovation leading to an inevitably self-destructive short-termism. Today, it has become perfectly normal to see objects disappear into garbage disposals and garage sales *as quickly as they appear on the market*.

(Hannah Arendt[9] and Günther Anders[10] both highlighted, each in their own style, the major questions raised by this obsolescence that destroys the sustainability of the world, and thus this world itself. Their arguments, however, which must be revisited from the perspective of their consequences for libidinal economy, largely ignored the organological and pharmacological dimension on which I would like here to insist, and therefore failed to open up any political or economic prospects.)

Generalized disposability, which has today been imposed throughout the world, and which affects human beings and businesses as much as the objects they produce, along with the ideas and concepts these objects incarnate and disincarnate, has installed a *systemic infidelity* orchestrated via marketing, and through which intergenerational relations have been inverted: children now dictate to parents how to behave – that is, what to buy.[11]

More generally, it is the entire *apparatus for the production of libidinal energy* – that is, for the diversion and trans-formation of drive-based ends (which are structurally short-term) into social investments crystallized in the form of primary and secondary identifications, *which presuppose idealizations and thus proteiform infinitizations* – it is this entire apparatus for the sublimatory production of libidinal energy that is being short-circuited and destroyed, along with desire and its objects, if not the Thing itself.

27.   The false self of the consumer without object

All societies have always been founded on the constitution of, and
by the rule of, fidelity and trust (these being the roots of the fiduciary dimension in monetary economies). Over the past century,
however, and perhaps fundamentally since the 'death of God', our
society has been based on developing infidelity: the systematic
organization of consumption presupposes *abandonment*; it presupposes abandoning objects, institutions, relations, places and
everything that it is possible for markets to control, all of which
must therefore be abandoned by the symbolic dimension [*le symbolique*], that is, de-symbolized.

This is the reign of adaptation, as Lyotard highlighted in *The
Postmodern Condition*, that is, in the language of Winnicott, of
the 'false self', of flexible becoming, and finally, in the language
of Zygmunt Bauman, of 'liquid society': the motto of liberalism
has become the liquidation of all relations of dependence created
by organizations of fidelity. Moreover, these relations of dependence founded on fidelity are being replaced by an organization
of *dependence grounded in infidelity* – in this case, in a *pharmacological dependence* on expedients (all objects becoming such
expedients, that is, substitutes for a lack that is no longer that of
the desiring subject but rather of the addict, made dependent by
their toxicomania).

All this results in *addicted consumers without object*: for without
objects to which they can attach themselves, given that the object
is that of a subject insofar as it supports a relation of attachment,
they endure the ordeal of the emptiness and futility of the self,
that is, the 'loss of the feeling of existing'.

Three remarks are necessary here:

1. The self as Winnicott tried to think it, which comes close to
   what Simondon conceptualized as psychic and collective
   individuation, is not reducible to the metaphysical self of
   consciousness: it is rather the self of the id, that is, of the
   unconscious. This is what must here be thought – and this
   necessarily involves a consideration of Bateson's theory of
   alcoholism.[12]
2. The systemic destruction of fidelity inevitably induced by permanent innovation and necessary to the consumerist economic

system also inevitably implies the systemic destruction of trust. No economic system can function, however, without an a priori basis in trust that it is the function of the fiduciary *hypomnematon* to stabilize, but that it cannot itself produce.

3. Such a basis is necessarily constituted by something incalculable, an improbability and an infinity, which was given, before His death, the name of God – and which also brought about, in the same stroke, when the nihilistic destiny of rationalization began to impose itself, the emergence of the Thing.

The systemic infidelity that destroys the transitionality of the object has its basis in an infidelity of the milieu that lies at the very basis of life. But in and as the *après-coup* of the doubly epokhal redoubling – as the second moment of the *pharmakon,* its curative moment, its normative remediation in the sense that it is inventive of a new system of care – this infidelity of the milieu, inherent to the evolution of life in totality and to the historicity of prosthetic life, presupposes the formation of a normativity of technical life, capable of turning the pharmacological pathology typical of that living thing who can 'want to be sick' into a new metastabilized milieu, or in other words a new space of fidelity: a *philia* opened *by a noesis.* This opening is what takes care of transitional space. It is precisely this transitionality of objects, and of the milieu that these objects form, that is destroyed by permanent innovation.

28. The first object of transindividuation

In the first volume of *Technics and Time,* I attempted to establish that the anthropological fact (the origin of hominization) lies in the constitution of an epiphylogenetic milieu: a milieu constituted by artefacts that become functional supports of a technical memory that is added to species memory (phylogenetic memory) and to the memory of the nervous system (epigenetic memory).

In order to become supports of memory, however, and to be internalized, and in order to constitute not only a memory but an imagination (that is, a power to figure and to schematize), these things, which 'spontaneously' constitute themselves into mnesic supports, must also be supports of *projection* – of the Thing, that is, of the default of origin (rather than of a simple lack) opening desire to the infinite and to the infinity of its objects, objects that substitute for the Thing, and of which things become the fetishes. Such a projection presupposes the formation of transitional space in Winnicott's sense of the term.

It used to be that the question of the *pharmakon*, the condition of the life of the spirit, even though it can just as well turn into its opposite (and, as we say colloquially in French, '*faire tourner en bourrique*', 'turn [someone] into an ass' [that is, drive them crazy]), was always set out on the basis of those *hypomnemata* that are the 'spiritual instruments', which is also to say, on the basis of the Platonic matrix of the problem of *hypomnesis*. Now:

1. The formation of things as epiphylogenetic supports occurs well before the emergence of hypomnesic supports strictly speaking;
2. A reading of Winnicott shows that it is a relation to an *initial* object, that is, a transitional object, and an object *that does not exist – no more than there has ever been an experience of the Thing* – that the primordial pharmacological process takes place;
3. Current child psychiatry, faced with the enormous pathogenic effects of the immersion of the infantile psychic apparatus in the audiovisual media pool, has over the past few years pointed out, notably in the work of Zimmerman and Christakis, this primordial role of the relation to transitional objects (that is, to the supports of motricity through which a world is opened up by being projected): the hyper-mediatized and hallucinatory milieu bypasses and short-circuits the sensori-motricity that Winnicott showed to be the condition of infantile psychogenesis.

It is the synaptogenesis of the child that is structurally altered by the immersion of its brain in the mediatized milieu. This modification of cerebral circuits is the internalization of a modification of social circuits – *for such is the brain: a relational organ that plastically internalizes social relational systems, systems that are themselves supported by the things, objects and artefacts that weave human commerce as experiences of the Thing.*

It is the internalization of social circuits within cerebral circuits that enables the constitution of transindividuation processes, that is, the formation of signification (of the transindividual). This signification constitutes the material of what Winnicott called creativity, which itself echoes what Canguilhem called normativity. And creativity is what produces meaning from significations shared by those who co-individuate themselves through a process of transindividuation.

During a transindividuation process, the co-individuation of many individuals tends to converge, beyond the differences of perspective between each individual, towards an attractor around which a metastable state of shared significations forms. These shared significations become the supports of interpretation, that is, of the production of meaning – one and the same signification, implicitly or explicitly accepted, can become in its play with other significations the vector of a new meaning, which is also to say, a transindividuation process for one or more new significations.

This movement of signification, within signification and beyond it, a movement that amounts to meaning, meaning being always tied to an emotion – signification is regulated and normal; meaning is unsettled and normative[13] – causes the transindividual to tend towards the plane of consistences: from the plane where signification establishes itself as definition (usage, rule), meaning inverts it by infinitizing it. Meaning only exists infinitely. It is in this way that convergences to the infinite form in the transindividual, and it is in this way that the transindividual opens existences to planes of consistence of objects that, like the Thing, do not exist.

Meaning and signification nevertheless only metastabilize and only deepen, only change phase, that is, only de-stabilize and potentialize, insofar as social and symbolic relations, within which they form and deform, are, ultimately, inscribed in neurons. Freud, in his *Project*, tried to think the dynamic elements of this process. Transindividuation is played out on the three levels of general organology simultaneously.

There is no process of transindividuation that is not dependent on exteriorization, which is itself artefactual and therefore technical – whether it is a matter of producing words, gestures, attitudes or any other form of expression or production. Such *expressivity* is, however, what affects and connects cerebral relational organs, in the interior of which, in other words, traces form (verbal or otherwise), and between which relations are metastabilized, which contribute in a general way to the formation of social organizations.

It could thus be said that the life of the brain to a large extent occurs *outside* the brain. But it has always also occurred *through* the brain – and pharmacological life has always been expressed in diverse neurochemical activities. Contemporary 'neurocentrism', which massively ignores this pharmacological dimension of life, has therefore been an obstacle to thinking the formation of meaning and signification: it reduces the human relational organ to its animal function – which is obviously an essential function, but one essentially devoted to the problem of subsistence. Neurocentrism has thus been an obstacle to understanding the noetic capacity of the brain.

29. The brain as living organ of transindividuation and the organology of spirit

Circuits of transindividuation, formed in the dialogism in which human commerce in general consists, are founded on a relation of *primordial trust* that, according to Winnicott's clinical analysis, is elaborated in early childhood through the experience of the transitional object. This space opens up a relation to consistences, that is, to what does not exist but consists: a relation to what 'makes life worth living'. Which is also to say: a relation to the Thing.

We have seen that the transitional object, that first *pharmakon*, founds everything that in adult life will constitute the objects of sublimation – that is, consistences. This presupposes the relation of care as learning or apprenticeship, that is, the experience and protection (by the mother) of that which does not exist, which is neither inside nor outside, as well as the encounter with consistence as such, that cultural and sublimatory life preserves and protects in its turn, and long circuits of transindividuation that extend infantile creativity and concretize adult normativity on the basis of *pharmaka*, *pharmaka* that may always also become supports of short-circuits, that is, of adaptive processes of disindividuation and of the formation of a false self.

The premature immersion of the child's psychic apparatus in the audiovisual pharmacological milieu short-circuits or bypasses this relation of care, and with it, the basis – as the synaptic translation of the relation to the 'mother' or her stand-in – of the formation of circuits of transindividuation that *link a social circuit and a cerebral circuit via the intermediary of a thing,* through which what Winnicott called a *relationship of care* is established, and through which the fundamental trust of the child is formed as the singularity of its relation to the Thing. This audiovisual pharmacological immersion cuts the child off from the transitional milieu and bars access to potential and transitional space, which is neither inside nor outside but constitutes a relational structure on the basis of which relations of trust and fidelity can be established.

The brain is a plastic space of reticulated inscriptions organized by the internalization and, if you will, the retro-projection of relations linked with and through the supports of epiphylogenetic projection – through which nervous memory both exteriorizes and internalizes itself, that is, weaves itself by passing through its outside, by making a detour through a pharmacological milieu – and such that synaptic short-circuits are also possible.

Transitional space is just as pharmacological as the audiovisual milieu, which is of course also, and even pre-eminently, a transitional space. But audiovisual transitional space is purely and simply toxic for the child's brain: if it were to eventually become curative this could only be on the basis of circuits formed by the motricity of the infantile transitional object.

These remarks are intended to emphasize that the history of the supplement foreshadowed by the logic of the supplement (also referred to as grammatology) presupposes a general organology of the mind or spirit that forms and deforms itself under pharmacological constraint and as a relation between the psychosomatic, technical and social organs that are linked together as transductive relations, that is, relations the terms of which are constituted by the relation itself. At the heart of this organology lies a genealogy of the sensible – and of the relation to the supra-sensible, which it is tempting to project here as the Thing itself – a genealogy that frames a relation to consistences, that is, to infinities.

This means that *the organology of the brain must apprehend this organ as the primary receptacle of grammatization* – where *the question of writing and of its psychic inscription, as well as of the inscription of verbal traces* (Saussure and Freud), is posed at a level *below* that of archi-writing, which is also to say, at a level below the topic of the 'quasi-transcendental' that laboriously accompanies it. Rather than focusing on the quasi-transcendental, it would be more fruitful to focus on potential or transitional space, which does not exist, being neither inside nor outside, but which consists – and projects that which makes life worthy of being lived.

Grammatization extends far beyond writing and *logos*. It concerns every process that 'discretizes' the continuous, notably those of gesture. As such, it describes both: the proletarianization of workers whose psycho-motor knowledge is discretized and captured by the machine, depriving them of their *savoir-faire*, their know-how; and the artificial audiovisual 'perception' that enables the analogical and then the digital discretization of the flux of images and sounds – doing so, however, by creating short-circuits, for example, those that ruin the relation of care and the formation of trust that provide access to consistences, by barring access to the infinities without which no trust is imaginable.

30.   As for the self – the pharmacology of the soul

As transitional support, every object is a *pharmakon* that induces the pharmacological constitution of those who live pharmacologically (*us*, affected by the Thing), so that it may stretch and sometimes tear the soul that is the psychic individual, with the result that, participating in collective individuation, it may disindividuate itself and in so doing disindividuate the collective, that is, damage it [*abîmer*], drive it towards the abyss [*vers l'abîme*]. For if there can be no psychic individuation without collective individuation, the converse is also true: there is no psychic disindividuation without collective disindividuation. This is what Winnicott called the *false self*. And this is in turn related to those questions that Plato raised in the *Gorgias*.

Does the false self presuppose a true self that would be 'authentic' or 'proper'? Clearly not: it is a *transitional* self, a relation woven beyond inside and outside, and that must be thought on the basis of a *pharmacology of the soul*. This is Simondon's central question in *L'individuation psychique et collective*: in that work, this question is presented as that of the indefinite dyad, that is, of a bipolarity that constitutes the play of tendencies throughout the psychic as well as the social individual, which in Simondon is presented as the ordeal of temptation.[14]

It is impossible to understand either the goodness or the evil of the soul, which are constitutive and dynamic tendencies (the dynamic of the drives, which supply energy to the libido, energy which is then dynamically 'diverted'), without taking these *pharmaka* into consideration, insofar as they can become either poisonous or curative and beneficial. Good and evil, goodness and wickedness, are pharmacological arrangements, and a person 'is' not good or evil – but all of us *become*, every day, by turns, according to fortune and mood (*Stimmung*), good or evil, representatives of goodness (that is, of nobility) or of wickedness (that is, of ignobility: vile).

The pharmacology of the soul is what Winnicott described as its originally transitional dimension, the transitional object being also the means of falsification of the self as circuit, that is, of the self as a relation for which the transitional object is the mediating factor. The human situation is *essentially* relational, and the psyche is formed relationally – that is, by inscribing itself on to circuits of transindividuation – on the basis of transitional (that is, technical and pharmacological) *facilitations*,[15] which presuppose mediators, *curators*, priests [*curés*] and therapists of all kinds.

As I have already emphasized, what Winnicott referred to as the environment, that is, transitional relational space, is here the crucial question:

> Freud used the word 'sublimation' to point the way to a place where cultural experience is meaningful, but perhaps he did not get so far as to tell us where in the mind cultural experience is.[16]
>
> Freud and Klein avoided [...] the full implication of dependence and therefore of the environmental factor.[17]

In other words, if there is a libidinal economy, it presupposes a libidinal ecology. The soul's goodness or wickedness, the false self

and the creative self, inhabit an intrinsically pathogenic pharmacological milieu. Or: psychogenesis is sociogenesis to the strict
extent that it is an irreducibly pharmacological technogenesis,
producing *pathos* and pathologies of all kinds.

31. The spirit of things and the pharmacological condition of nihilism

As environment the relational fabric is what ties together, through
transitional and pharmacological mediations, a physiology, a
history and a geography of the spirit. Circuits of transindividuation are circuits of desire, that is, circulations of intensities that
traverse and form by opening up [*frayant*] networks – just as paths
open up, and just as movement shows: by moving. Through
this, relations of attachment, *philia*, projections, identifications,
acknowledgements, obligations and so on, are tied together, but
also deadlocks, imprisonments, boundaries and borders delimiting
territories.

The pharmacology of the spirit is a pharmacology of *symbolic*
relations, but within which objects are the primary instances,
and where what the Greeks called the *sumbolon* is an object. Prior
to being constituted hypomnesically, the circuits of transindividuation whereby a mind is formed deploy themselves on the basis
of infantile transitional relations, and as objects *invested with
spirit* in the sense given to this phrase by Husserl, who referred
firstly to books, but extended its use to all common objects: 'a
drinking glass, a house, a spoon, theatre, temple'[18] were Husserl's
examples of the way that familiar objects are always already spiritual objects.

There are, however, epochs and a genealogy to be established
for these objects invested with spirit – on the basis of the infantile
transitional object – through which spiritual and pharmacological
configurations are formed. Without this genealogy of the sensible,
without the concepts of general organology, and without the
process of grammatization that deploys itself within it, and that
constitutes the *pre-eminently pharmacological condition of nihilism*, that is, both the death of God and the re-valuation of all
values, it will not be possible to think contemporary *kenosis* – that
is, to overcome it.

Within these epochs, there are objects invested with *those* spirits that, in Melanesia and New Zealand, create intensities that Melanesians and Maoris call *mana* and *hau*. *Mana* can be fixed upon an object, as if the object were able to carry the power of *mana*:

> *Mana* is not simply a force, a being, it is also an action, a quality, a state. [...] One says of an object that it is *mana*, in order to refer to this quality. [...] People say that a being, a spirit, a man, a stone or a rite *has mana*, 'the *mana* to do such and such a thing'. [...] The word covers a host of ideas which we would designate by phrases such as a sorcerer's power, the magical quality of a thing, a magical thing...[19]

As such, *mana* erases boundaries and constitutes in magical society a kind of *transitional phenomenon on the scale of social relations* – just as practices of sublimation preserve a transitional space in adult social life, as Winnicott has shown. *Mana* 'shows this confusion of actor, rite and things that seems to be fundamental to magic'.[20]

What the Maori tribes refer to with the word *hau*, which is transmitted through exchanged objects and which transforms them so that only thus do they *become* objects, is an exchange of *taonga*, that is, an exchange of items in the sense one says about the items found in stores – if not an exchange of merchandise, which is a word that Mauss hesitates to use precisely because, in this case, there is no market.

There is, however, a constitution of relations of *obligation*, and therefore the creation of a social bond through which the social group is formed:

> The *taonga* and all goods termed strictly personal possess a *hau*, a spiritual power. You give me one of them, and I pass it on to a third party; he gives another to me in turn, because he is impelled to do so by the *hau* my present possesses. I, for my part, am obliged to give you that thing because I must return to you what is in reality the effect of the *hau* of your *taonga*. [...] What imposes obligation in the present received and exchanged, is the fact that the thing received is not inactive. Even when it has been abandoned by the giver, it still possesses something of him. Through it the giver has

a hold over the beneficiary just as, being its owner, through it he has a hold over the thief.[21]

32. Industrial *kenosis* and economy of the infinite

The seal hunter who carves his harpoon pursues the formation of his transitional space and thereby enters into a relation with himself such as the spirits destine him to enter – and with the seals, too, insofar as they are themselves spirits. Is this relational dimension superfluous and reducible, or on the contrary constitutive of the symbolic and the imaginary?

In sedentary society, far removed from this hunter, from these seals and spirits, already urban but still ancient, things, having become products of the division of labour, take the form of merchandise, placing those who acquire them into a relation with other psychic individualities who have made them – the craftsmanship involved in what was created by so-called artisans configured a worldhood that constituted a society that today we consider to be traditional, even though it was urban. This division of labour remained a relational space of transmission, according to methods such as rules of life, and formed a 'tradition' insofar as these rules were co-elaborated by those who lived them.

With the commencement of the Industrial Revolution, craftsmanship and handicraft [*la facture et la manufacture*] begin to be replaced by the factory, where it is the machine-tool that produces things: these things become objects of a process of technological rationalization and mass production that results in standardization. This leads after the Second World War to consumerism on a planetary scale, based on the model elaborated in the United States, the consumer object penetrating society on the basis of socialization policies that operate via marketing, which takes away from society the possibility of defining social practices – of which things would be the supports. This period that began with the Industrial Revolution presupposes a process of the grammatization of production methods, bypassing the 'thingly' knowledge of workers who thus become proletarians: their knowledge passes into machines, and so too with the loss of their knowledge goes the relational and transitional modes and methods of which this knowledge was the psychic internalization.

Currently, a new milieu is developing, the digital milieu, and this is a new stage of grammatization, bringing with it new relations not only between subjects, who have become 'internauts' and 'digital natives', but between objects, forming an 'internet of things'.

After the 'death of God', the pharmacological beings that we are:

- discovered the unconscious and the Thing it harbours; and
- underwent the disenchantment of the world, which suggests we should *rethink kenosis.*

The absolute reign of *ratio* as the finitization of the world tends to reduce, via calculation, everything that proceeds along that other plane constitutive of objects of desire in all their forms, forming precisely so many figures and schemas of infinity: having become a libidinal diseconomy,[22] consumerist capitalism systemically destroys all objects of desire. And such objects, belonging to the potential space of objects that do not exist, can spontaneously infinitize themselves only by being kept on paths of transindividuation – this is what I call care.

Finitization, which bypasses or short-circuits these paths, is simply a fact, and if this includes the fact of a consumerist economy grounded in negligence and carelessness [*incurie*], *it is also the fact of the carelessness of infinitizing thought (that is, noetic thought)* in the face of a pharmacological situation that is awaiting a therapeutic.

The thought of desire and of the Thing, which is not a thought of 'lack' but of default, that is, of the *pharmakon,* is a thought that remains yet to come: it is the question par excellence of a century – ours – that has not begun well. It is the question of that *which does not exist,* but which, inspiring trust, ties together relations of fidelity in this *economy of the infinite* that is the only economy of true value, that is, an economy which is not just sustainable but in principle '*to the infinite*' – and which makes life worth living beyond the calculating fiduciary system which *ratio* (reason) has become in *all* its forms.

After the death of God, that is, after the *kenotic ordeal of the fact that what consists does not exist,* or in other words after

Freud, the infinitude of the object of desire points to an altogether other *domain*, which is *secret* and certainly taboo, if not sacred: the unconscious. It is this aspect of the psychic apparatus that Freud's nephew promoted as the foundational element of consumerism,[23] and through which disenchantment was accelerated.

This may translate into the destruction of transitional 'creativity' (in Winnicott's sense), or 'normativity' (in Canguilhem's sense), which are individuating and productive of desire, that is, of infinity. The systemic obsolescence and infidelity that is spread by a grammatization *which remains unthought and thus essentially careless* short-circuits the process of transindividuation and produces generalized proletarianization and disindividuation, draining or emptying the apparatus for production of libido (insofar as this binds the drives), and through this the transitional, that is, the pharmacological, has become a purely adaptive support, and one which finds itself constantly becoming obsolete.

33. Rock bottom: techniques of the self and others as the power to infinitize and to know infinitely

Disenchantment as the calculation of trust, and as fiduciary calculation, leads to the liquidation of fidelity, friendship, love, *philia*, knowledge, arts and letters, in a word, of what makes life worth living. Now, I have taken the risk, with *Ars Industrialis*, of getting behind the following infinitive: '*to re-enchant*' the world – that is, to invert the kenotic horizon that is the nihilism of the prosthetic god, of a pharmacology soliciting the drives, turning it instead into a new therapeutic that re-invests the *pharmakon* as remedy, cure, transitional mediation understood as transindividuation – to re-enchant this world confronted with a new pharmacology constituted by the digital milieu, its relational technologies and its completely *revolutionary* social practices.

What did we mean by saying that we risked this *infinitive* statement, that is, one that in French begins with an infinitive *verb*? We wanted to say above all that *no existence is possible without infinity*, and more precisely, without that which *grants the power to infinitize* – which in turn presupposes *knowing how* to infinitize.

Nihilism is both an historical necessity[24] and what Nietzsche announced as the *bottom touched* by the pharmacological beings that we are, like those alcoholics that according to Alcoholics Anonymous will only want to cure themselves when they have hit bottom[25] – those who in earlier days were called *sinners*, according to a Manichean conception holding that *sin* was *the flaw conceived and suffered as what ought not be.*

The bottom, or as it is said in English, 'rock bottom'. This is what is happening to us, and it is also the title of a wonderful collection of music that Robert Wyatt wrote, sang and recorded in 1974, accompanied by trumpeter Monguezi Feza, a year after taking LSD and falling from a window, which cost him the use of his legs.

34. Libidinal ecology of infinite immanence

After the discovery of the unconscious, which is also to say, the discovery of the Thing, the *default* (rather than a 'lack') that the Thing proves to be is the *pharmakon* as transitional object and *condition of infinitization* in the relation of care that is desire and its formation, that is, the constitution of a libidinal economy that, as the elaboration and transmission of knowing how to infinitize, inverts the destructive economy of drives by diverting their ends. The *default* becomes *that which is necessary*, that is, that *of* which, like the Thing, we must take care.

It appears, then, that nihilism must be understood as a historial process traversing and weaving a process of divestment [*dépouillement*] through grammatization, that is, a process of *pharmacological kenosis*. Grammatization is always *above all* the destruction of circuits of desire, that is, the destruction of the power to infinitize and of the knowledge that this presupposes and makes possible.[26] But it is also always what *constitutes* new knowledge and new powers, *après-coup*, as new therapeutics emerge from the new pharmacology in which a new stage of grammatization consists.

During the monotheistic age, faced with a *pharmakon* understood as sin, the sinner would think and live infinity as transcendence, that is, as *supreme existence* and as the ontotheology of the *summum ens*. The re-valuation of all values inscribes the possibility of infinitization – the power to infinitize and infinitizing-knowledge – in an immanence without transcendence, yet as a new horizon of consistences.

If Nietzsche argued that with the death of God so too the suprasensible is liquidated, this was because he saw it as related to the intelligible that Plato *opposed* to the sensible. And in Christian ontotheology the intelligible, as a world-beyond founded in the *realism* of ideas, becomes the *existence* of God, that is, of the *improbable* that it is still a matter of *proving* exists, at the risk of ruining all consistence.

After Freud, the infinite becomes the object of desire *that clearly does not exist* – and that, if one can put it like this, *does not exist infinitely*. Such is *das Ding*: the Thing. After the twentieth century – which exploited the Freudian discovery to the point of emptying it of its very object, the *kenosis* of the transitional object being engulfed and dissolved by the obsolescence of all things; and in the pharmacological context of digital transitional space characteristic of the twenty-first century – it is the economy of the object of desire that must be reconstructed as libidinal ecology, from and as a new critique of the politico-libidinal economy of sublimation and of contemporary transitional milieus.[27]

The question of the infinite has become the question par excellence of political economy.

When the question of the infinite becomes that of immanence itself – insofar as, being both symbolic and imaginary, it is constituted by a process of transindividuation of which things, as transitional objects, that is, as *pharmaka*, are the condition of possibility (of consistence) as well as of impossibility (of inexistence) – then the question of desire and of the care taken of its object, of which *philia, eros, agape, charis*, love and sublimation are names, and the supports of the fidelity that gathers them together, this question of desire becomes not only the object of libidinal economy understood as a therapeutic organization of pharmacology, but the question of a new critique of political economy conceived as a pharmacology of capital.

Part III

Pharmacology of Capital

5

Economizing Means Taking Care: The Three Limits of Capitalism

35. Psychic apparatus and social apparatus in the 'attention economy'

The future of the planet must be thought from the question of psychopower characteristic of control societies, the effects of which have become massive and destructive. Globalized psychopower is the systematic organization of the capture of attention made possible by the psychotechnologies that have developed with radio (1920), television (1950) and digital technologies (1990). It has spread across the surface of the planet via several forms of networks, producing a constant industrial channelling of attention, and resulting in a new phenomenon: a massive destruction of attention, referred to by nosologists in the United States as 'attention deficit disorder'. This destruction of attention is a particular, and particularly severe, case of the destruction of libidinal energy through which the capitalist libidinal economy is destroying itself.

Attention is the reality of individuation understood in Simondon's sense, that is, insofar as it is always both psychic and collective. Attention is the psychic faculty that allows us to concentrate on an object, that is, to give ourselves over to an object, but it is also the social faculty that allows us to take care of this object – or of another, or of the representative of another, or of the object of the other: attention is also the name of that civility that is grounded in *philia*, that is, socialized libidinal energy.

This is why the destruction of attention implies the destruction of both the *psychic apparatus* and the *social apparatus* (formed through collective individuation), insofar as the latter constitutes a system of care, given that to pay attention is also to take care. Such a system of care is also a libidinal economy, through which a psychic apparatus and a social apparatus are connected together, but today we find that *technological apparatus* is destroying this economy. And, as we shall see, this also involves psychotechnological and sociotechnological apparatus. In other words, this question relates to what I refer to as 'general organology'.

The main question that arises from attention deficit disorder, and from the results of the destructive effects of the exploitation of attention by psychopower, derives from the fact that the infantile psychic apparatus is weakened and made fragile, as is that sociability grounded in *philia*. Now, this premature liquidation of libidinal economy also destroys industrial capitalism insofar as it is based on *investment*: the organ of psychopower is marketing, which is the armed wing of a financialized capitalism that has become essentially speculative.

36. The grammatization of transindividuation itself and the passage from psychotechnologies to sociotechnologies

The enormous financial crisis that has shaken the whole world, and the various ongoing and ever more disturbing effects resulting from the 'remedies' tried by governments, are all the disastrous result of the hegemony of the short term, of which the destruction of attention is both an effect and a cause. The loss of attention is a loss of the capacity to project into the long term (that is, to invest in objects of desire) that *systemically* affects the psychic apparatus of those consumers manipulated by psychopower, but equally affects the manipulators themselves: speculators are typically people who pay little attention to the objects of their speculation – and who, moreover, take little care of them.

The actions of speculators have effects on the multitude of consciousnesses that suffer – directly or indirectly – the effects of speculation through the psychotechnological systems that capture their attention. These consciousnesses find themselves ever more enclosed within a lack of attention and care, *that is, within the short term*. And this *justifies a posteriori* the actions of the speculator: the speculative act is performative in the sense given to this word by Jean-François Lyotard in *The Postmodern Condition*. In this way a system based on the short term is established – bringing about a vicious circle that destroys attention.

It is in this context that a colossal environmental crisis rages on, a crisis that has been placed on the top rung of global concern (*Besorgen*) and attention (*Sorge*) by the Nobel Academy. A third limit of capitalism has thereby been discovered and globally recognized – after the tendency of the rate of profit to fall, and the tendency of libidinal energy to fall (which is the direct result of the destruction of attention).

In this context of environmental crisis, which suddenly makes the need for long-term thinking seem so clear, that is, the need to re-elaborate a politics of investment – at the precise moment when an enormous financial crisis has exposed the calamity of the speculative and short-termist organization induced by the financialization that destroys attention – new operations of spectacular industrial concentration are being implemented or prepared: Google has drawn most of the focus in this regard, by having crossed an immeasurable threshold to the industrialization of psychic and collective memory.

The goal of such operations is to take control of socio-digital networks deploying those new ways of capturing and forming psychic and collective attention that are 'social networks': a *new age of reticulation* is being implemented, and it constitutes a new stage of the grammatization process. In this stage, *it is the mechanisms of transindividuation itself that are grammatized*, that is, formalized and made reproducible, and therefore capable of being calculated and automated. Now, transindividuation is the way in which psychic individuations are meta-stabilized as collective individuation: transindividuation is the operation of the fully actualized socialization of the psychic.

With the advent of 'social networks' the question of attentional technologies has manifestly and explicitly become the question of transindividuation technologies. Transindividuation is now

formalized through the use of psychic individuation technologies
originally conceived in order to achieve collective individuation,
spectacularly and organologically confirming the Simondonian
analysis according to which psychic individuation is also and
immediately collective individuation. This involves technologies of
indexation and annotation, as well as tags and modelled traces,[1]
wikis and collaborative technologies in general.[2]

Here, a reading of Foucault is especially necessary and productive: Foucault showed in his reading of the correspondence between
Seneca and Lucilius that techniques of the self, as techniques of
psychic individuation, are always already techniques of collective
individuation. Foucault was unable to foresee, however, the question of psychopower: marketing, beginning with the emergence of
the programme industries, has transformed the psychotechniques
of the self and psychic individuation into industrial psychotechnologies of transindividuation, that is, into psychotechnologies
woven through networks, and has done so as the organization of
an industrial reticulation of transindividuation that short-circuits
and bypasses traditional and institutional social networks.

Having destroyed traditional social networks, psychotechnologies have become sociotechnologies, and they tend to form
themselves into a new milieu and a new reticular condition of
transindividuation that grammatizes new forms of social
relations.

37.   Tertiary retention and transindividuation

In order to analyse these developments, which constitute the specific context in relation to which it is necessary and possible to
think a future for the planet, we must return to the question of
what attention actually is. Psychic *and* collective individuation is
essentially what forms attention insofar as it is necessarily both
psychic and social, and attention is what results from the relation
between retention and protention in the Husserlian sense of these
terms (what Husserl called intentional consciousness is what I am
calling attention).[3] Now, this relation between retention and protention, the result of which is attention, is always mediated by
tertiary retention – of which psychotechnologies and sociotechnologies are instances.

If we are to complete the analysis in which Husserl distinguished primary retention from secondary retention, we must refer to tertiary retention. Primary retention is, for example, what occurs when someone listens to another person speak and, relating the verb used by the speaker back to the subject that preceded it, a word that is no longer being perceived directly, the listener maintains this subject in the verb, which constitutes the maintenance of the speaker's discourse as well as the listener's attention: the listener conjugates the subject to the verb, with a view to projecting this action designated by the verb towards its complement. This projection is a protention, that is, an expectation.

What Husserl called primary retention is this operation that consists in retaining one word within another word (an operation that Husserl analysed by studying the way that in a melody one note retains within it the note that preceded it, and projects forward the expectation of a further note, which Leonard Meyer described as an expectation). This operation consists, then, in retaining a word that is no longer present: the beginning of the sentence has already been uttered and is as such already past, and yet it *is* still present in the *meaning* that unfolds as speech.

We must distinguish the *operation* that is primary retention from secondary retention. A secondary retention is a memory, something that belongs to a past that has passed by (it is thus a former primary retention), whereas primary retention still belongs to the present, to a passing present: it is the very passage and as such the direction of the present – thus also its meaning, in terms of its sense of direction. Memory as secondary retention is also what enables us to select from among possibilities in primary retention: primary retention is a primary *selection*, and the criteria for this selection are furnished by secondary retention (by memories, that is, individual experience).

Imagine we are at a conference, and that I am delivering the sentences that are written here on this page. This was in fact the case in April 2008 at the University at Albany, State University of New York, where I was invited by Tom Cohen for a symposium organized by the Institute on Critical Climate Change,[4] at which I made the following remarks.

You are all listening to me, but each of you hears what I say differently, and this is because your secondary retentions are

singular: your pasts are singular. By the same token, your understanding of what I say is each time singular: the meaning you
assign to my discourse, through which you individuate yourself
with my discourse, is each time singular – and this is the case
because you are singularly selecting primary retentions of the
discourse I am delivering to you, a discourse through which I am
trying to retain and maintain your attention.

If, however, you were now able to repeat this whole speech
that you have just listened to, if, for example, you had recorded
it on to a memory stick as an MP3 file, you would obviously
bring about new primary retentions, and you would do so in
relation to the preceding primary retentions that have in the
meantime become secondary retentions. You would therefore
reconsider the meaning of this discourse as you had previously
constituted it: through this repetition you would produce a
difference in meaning, through which this meaning reveals
itself to be more a process than a state. More precisely, it reveals
itself to be *the process of your own individuation* arranging itself
with the individuation that this discourse testifies to, which in
this case is my own individuation. You would thereby form
retentional circuits that are at the origin of new circuits of
transindividuation.

Be that as it may, what enables the repetition of a speech, in
the form for example of an MP3 recording, is tertiary retention,
just as the written text that I am now reading to you allows me
to repeat a discourse that I conceived elsewhere, at an earlier time:
it is a hypomnesic *pharmakon*. Such a *pharmakon* enables *attentional effects* to be produced, that is, retentional and protentional
arrangements, the existence of which entirely justifies the definition of this *pharmakon* as a psychotechnical system or device.
Such a device allows, more precisely, the control of retentional
and protentional arrangements with the aim of producing
attentional effects.

Such effects are also those analysed by Husserl as the condition
of the origin of geometry – where writing is what enabled the
formation of rational types of primary and secondary retention,
through which long circuits of transindividuation could be formed,
including those denounced by Plato in the *Phaedrus* and in *Gorgias*
on the grounds that these intermediate, tertiary, hypomnesic

retentions make it possible to bypass or short-circuit the anamnesic work of thinking.

Tertiary retentions are therefore mnemotechnical forms of the exteriorization of psychic life constituting traces organized through retentional devices and systems (of which the systems described by Foucault in *The Order of Things*, *The Archaeology of Knowledge* and *Discipline and Punish* are cases), and attention is *conditioned* by these retentional systems – which characterize systems of care, as therapeutic systems of which retentional systems are the pharmacological basis.

Now, retentional systems and devices are at present entering into a new *distributed organization* that in fact represents a major rupture with the preceding organization of industrial society.[5] This rupture represents a crossroads in relation to which a new industrial politics must make choices and draw consequences, and it is only on this basis that new solutions may be found for the problems of the hyperindustrial world. This is an opportunity but at the same time a new danger (it is induced by a new *pharmakon*), and it has arisen at the very moment that capitalism finds itself confronted by three limits.

38. The three limits of capitalism and the question of care

Capitalism encountered its first two limits at the end of the nineteenth century and the end of the twentieth century respectively.

The Industrial Revolution, as the implementation of the capitalist system of production, continued the process of grammatization through which tertiary retentions were formed – including psychotechniques – via apparatus devised to control gestures. This apparatus, in the form of machine-tools, enabled the elimination of the *savoir-faire*, the skill and know-how, of workers, and thereby made possible the achievement of immense gains in productivity and new levels of prosperity, but it nevertheless encountered, beyond the misery and poverty it produced in the form of the proletariat, that limit analysed by Marx as the tendency of the profit rate to fall.[6]

As a way of struggling against this limit of capitalist development, the 'American way of life' invented the figure of the

consumer whose libido is systematically solicited in order to coun-
teract the threat of overproduction, which is the concrete social
expression of the tendency of the profit rate to fall. This channelling of the libido that works by capturing and harnessing attention
ends in the elimination of the *savoir-vivre* of consumers, through
the massive development of service-based societies that discharge
them of the obligations of their own existences, that is, of their
responsibilities as mature adults. In the end, this results in the
elimination of their own desire as well as the desire of their own
children, to the strict extent that the latter can no longer identify
with them, both because these parents no longer know anything,
and are no longer responsible for anything, having themselves
become overgrown children, and also because the process of
primary identification has been short-circuited by the psychopower of psychotechnologies.

This destruction of desire (which is also to say, of attention and
care), which leads to a drive-based economy, that is, an essentially
destructive economy, is a new limit encountered by capitalism,
this time not only as mode of production but also as mode of
consumption defined as way of life, that is, as *biopower become
psychopower.*

A *third limit* is now imposing itself, deriving from the fact that
the development of the industrial way of life, inherited from the
nineteenth and twentieth centuries, has become toxic not only on
the plane of minds and libido, but also on the geophysical and
biological plane.

This third limit can only be overcome on the condition of
inventing a way of life that constitutes a new way of taking care
of the world, a new way of paying attention to it, through the
invention of therapeutics: techniques, technologies and sociophar-
macological apparatuses of the formation of attention correspond-
ing to the organological specificities of our age. They must
correspond to the specificities of transindividuation technologies
that will form the infrastructure of an industrial system itself
functioning *in an endogenous fashion* as a system of care, *making
care its 'value chain', that is, its economy* – and thereby recon-
necting to the original meaning of the word 'economy', for *to
economize is to take care.*

39. Reinvestment

Western societies are undergoing the effects of the fact that technologies that originated from their own mode of production have now been exported, giving rise to industrial competitors (Paul Valéry already reflected on the consequences of this, even though at that time they remained yet to come) through a movement towards financialization that inevitably unleashes a global economic war.

In this *new form of war*, it is no longer a matter of defending society against an 'enemy', whether external or internal. Rather, it is a matter of defending society against a *process* that ruins time, that is, the horizon of the long term, and the possibility of projecting this horizon and at the same time projecting intergenerational relations – which are the condition of the attention given to objects of desire. This process is spinning out of control at the very moment that the effects of the three limits of capitalism are combining.

Global competition has been intensified by financialization, resulting in the destruction of the complex equilibrium that made it possible for the development of capitalism to also involve the social development of industrial democracies via the Keynesian organization of the redistribution of wealth under the authority of a welfare state. And it is in the context of the resulting economic war that marketing has become, as Gilles Deleuze wrote, 'the instrument of social control' in control societies, and that the fall in libidinal energy has suddenly worsened.

It is in this way that, in terms of consumption and at the end of the twentieth century, the capitalist way of life became an addictive process less and less capable of bringing sustainable satisfaction. The result has been high levels of discontent in relation to consumption, which has replaced culture, that is, care, given that culture proceeds from cults of all types, that is, attachments to objects that, taken as a totality, constitute a system of care. It is in this context that Jenny Uechi could write in *Abdusters*:

> According to recent surveys by sociologist Juliet Schor, 81 per cent of Americans believe their country is too focused on shopping, while nearly 90 per cent believe it is too materialistic.

We all know that in no case will this new global capitalism be able to develop by reproducing the modes of production and consumption that have been characteristic of Western, Japanese and Korean industrial democracies. For to export this way of life would be to also export the growth in the production of toxins of all kinds to the great majority of the planetary population, the result of which could well lead to the disappearance of the human race – to say nothing of the destruction of psychic apparatuses that also has effects that spread as quickly as this 'growth', which is in reality, and for this very reason, a *mis-growth* [*mécroissance*]. The new global capitalism will be capable of *renewing its energies* only on the condition that it invents a *new logic and new objects of investment* – and here the word investment must be taken in the widest sense: in the sense both of industrial economy and libidinal economy.

40. What is 'energy policy'?

In a text devoted to European energy policy, Jeremy Rifkin,[7] placing his discourse under the sign of the 'end of the age of oil', asks how we are to ensure 'sustainable development'. He does so, however, without ever posing the problem of mis-growth, that is, 'growth' that destroys desire, and that disindividuates producers as well as consumers, ruining the dynamism of what Max Weber called the spirit of capitalism, a spirit that must be understood as a libidinal energy that can be constituted only through the kinds of sublimation processes that are now being annihilated by marketing.

Although Rifkin never raises these questions (which were nevertheless the horizon of his works, *The European Dream* and *The Age of Access*), he does emphasize, in relation to the age of oil and of fossil fuels generally, that there are growing 'external costs' (which economists refer to as negative externalities). He does, then, implicitly refer to the third limit encountered by a capitalism that has become an *effectively globalized* technological system of production and consumption. In this context, he writes, there may be a residual stock of fossil energy that we will need to learn to exploit to the maximum, that is, in the

most economical way possible, but at the same time other processes for the production and consumption of energy will need
to be implemented: 'Looking to the future, every government
will need to explore new energy paths and establish new economic models.'[8]

It is indeed a matter of changing the economic model. But the
heart of this question is not that of the energy needed for subsistence: the true question concerns that energy of *existence* that is
libidinal energy.

By only posing the question of new ways of producing renewable subsistence energy such as those based on using hydrogen
technology as a storage medium, however, Rifkin would have us
believe that the energy crisis is temporary and that we will be able
to overcome it, and with it the third limit of capitalism, and that
all this will be possible without having to pose the question of
libidinal energy, without taking into account this second limit that
is in fact the truth of the third: the fact that the libido is being
destroyed, and that the drives it contained (like a Pandora's box
holding within it every evil) now rule over beings devoid of
attention, and incapable of taking care of their world.

Libidinal energy is essentially renewable, except when it
decomposes into drive-based energy, which on the contrary
destroys its objects. The drives are indeed energy, but they are
essentially destructive, because the drive *consumes its object*
[*consomme son objet*], which means that it eats away at it
[*qu'elle le consume*]. This consumption [*cette consumption et
cette consumation*], implemented by *consumers*, is a destruction.
Consummare, which is the origin of the verb 'to consume', and
which initially meant to complete, to reach a goal, becomes
with Christianity a synonym of 'to lose', *perdere*, and to destroy,
destruere. Beginning in 1580, the French verb *consommer* meant
to use up food and energy. We begin to hear about 'consumers'
from around 1745, and *consommation* then referred to the use
made of something in order to satisfy needs. Consumption
became a central economic term at the beginning of the twentieth century. And it was in 1972 that the word *consumerism*
appeared in the United States.

41. Energy of subsistence, energy of existence and new savoir-vivre

If consumption destroys its object, libido is on the contrary what *takes care* of its object. And this is why addressing the third limit of capitalism does not imply abandoning fossil energy but rather abandoning a drive-based economy and reconstituting libidinal energy, which is a form of renewable energy – given that *frequenting the objects of this energy causes it to increase.* The third limit of capitalism is not just a matter of the depletion of fossil fuel reserves: it is the limit constituted by the drive to destroy all objects in general through consumption, insofar as they have become objects of the drives rather than objects of desire and attention – the psychotechnological organization of consumption destroys attention in all its forms, on the psychic plane as well as the collective plane.

Rifkin, then, seems to completely ignore the second limit of capitalism and the meaning it acquires when the third limit has been reached, and for this reason his discourse seems to me to be fraught with danger: he would have us believe that drive-based growth could be sustained with the help of hydrogen technology. Despite this, Rifkin's account is interesting and important for at least three reasons:

1. On the one hand, he proposes a real alternative to the problem of subsistence energy, with his proposal for a hydrogen-based system that would allow a harmful limit to be pushed back.
2. On the other hand, he posits that questions of energy are never distinct from questions of communication and information networks, that is, hypomnesic systems, retentional systems of tertiary retentions.
3. Finally, and above all, he posits that the hydrogen network must be based on the model of social networks made possible by the World Wide Web and, thus, *must surpass the opposition between production and consumption.*

Consumption-based organization, constituted by the opposition of production and consumption, is dangerous not only because it produces excess carbon dioxide but because it destroys minds

and spirits. The consequence of opposing production and consumption is that both producers and consumers are proletarianized by the loss of their knowledge: they are reduced to an economy
of subsistence, and deprived of any economy of their existence –
they are deprived of libidinal economy, that is, of desire. This is
why the fundamental question raised by the combination of the
three limits of capitalism is that of overcoming this opposition and
the proletarianization it structurally engenders.

What is extremely interesting is Rifkin's proposition that energy
systems and information or mnemotechnical systems co-develop,
and that the most recent communication system, the Internet,
breaks, precisely, with the opposition between consumption and
production, and therefore constitutes the possibility of implementing a new distributed and decentralized network of renewable
energy in which everyone would be both producer and consumer
– by combining hydrogen storage technology with networks
based on the Internet model.

The application of this contributory model to the energy sector
results in what is referred to as 'smart grids'. Various models of
such energy networks already exist: these are not yet based on
hydrogen storage, but they are characterized by an organization
of production that is decentralized and distributed throughout
the network.

Confronted with this unprecedented challenge facing globalized
humanity – a challenge of almost sublime dimensions, requiring
an extraordinary mobilization of the forces of mind and spirit to
meet it, a challenge convoking what Kant called the suprasensible,
which is also to say, the infinite (infinitely renewable) – the temptation of the industrial and capitalist world has been to offer a
technological and scientific response that denies the three limits
of capitalism. This temptation grounded in denial fails to
comprehend:

1. That these three limits, when they combine, produce a systemic
   evolution at a higher level, that is, they cause something to
   emerge.
2. That the industrial model must be changed not simply in order
   to produce a new technical and scientific rationality, but to
   constitute a new social rationality, producing motivation,

motives for living together, that is, for taking care of the world
and those who live within it – producing a new *savoir-vivre*.
3. That the fundamental issue is here to reorient financial flows
   towards long-term investment by waging war against speculation – but also against ways of life founded on the short term,
   of which the most everyday example is the organization of
   society through marketing, in a way that systematically
   exploits the drives by destroying the libido as the *capacity
   for sustainable investment*.

When consumption becomes drive-based, society is profoundly
endangered. If there were no limit to this consumption, and if
fossil energy was inexhaustible, the catastrophe would perhaps be
even greater than the one resulting from the depletion of fossil
fuels. *Perhaps this depletion is in the end a kind of chance*: the
opportunity to understand that the true question of energy lies
elsewhere, that subsistence energy is only useful to the extent that
it contributes to an energy of existence – and does so through its
capacity to *project* the plane of consistences. Such are the true
stakes involved in what is referred to today, somewhat question-
ably, as 'ascending innovation'.

42. Political technologies and the transindividuation of disputes

Over the last ten years, society as a whole (in industrialized countries and industrializing countries) – thanks to a spectacular drop
in the costs of the electronic technologies used to fabricate materials, and in the costs of data transactions and copying – has
acquired new practical competencies, but also analytical and
reflexive competencies, through the growth of digital apparatus
that grants access to functionalities hitherto reserved for professionals, and hitherto organized according to an industrial division of labour (and everything that comes with it, such as, for
example, intellectual property laws).

This socialization of innovation more and more frequently
engages social forms of apprenticeship that seem to be self-
organizing and to elude the more usual process of socializing
innovation referred to as 'descending' (steered by the research/

development/marketing complex): instead we find what is referred to as 'ascending' innovation. Ascending innovation is a structural break with that organization of social relations in the industrial world that operates according to the opposing couple, 'production/consumption'.

Pour en finir avec la mécroissance tried to show that the opposition between 'bottom-up' and 'top-down' transindividuation processes is an illusion, that is, an unsustainable state of affairs – but a state of affairs that is, however, exploited by marketing and the culture industries, which appropriate collaborative media by using 'buzz' and other control and fabrication techniques deriving from what Bernays named 'public relations', an exploitation that establishes pseudo-contributive situations.

This work also related the individual practices and new social movements emerging from digital networks to attempts to take care of the self and others, and to those techniques of the self that were the *epimeleai, skhole* and *otium* of the Ancients, all of which were also techniques of governmentality.

Rather than opposing the 'bottom-up' to the 'top-down', it is a matter of constituting systems for producing metadata[9] that organize and create political technologies encouraging the emergence of psychic and collective individuation processes of a new kind. These systems must be grounded in the representation of differing perspectives, polemics and controversies, as well as convergences of interest or perspective enabling re-groupings, that is, ultimately, transindividuations that recognize themselves in meanings, thereby constituting collective individuations, and establishing, at the heart of digitalized public life, argued and analysable critique that counters the murmurings that abound in a falsely consensual digital world lacking instruments for enhancing collective singularities.

Digital technologies form *a new technological milieu that is reticulated and relational*, related to what Simondon called an 'associated techno-geographic milieu'. These technologies reconfigure what Simondon called the process of psychic and collective individuation, and transform into technologies of the spirit what have hitherto functioned essentially as technologies of control.

In this technological milieu, electronic apparatus has been connected into a system, via the network that formed thanks to the

IP protocol. The resulting dynamic system is in constant evolution and is grounded in a relational economy of miniaturized and personalized equipment and relational services – referred to, notably by Jeremy Rifkin, as relational technologies (or 'R technologies').

This system brings with it new social dynamics, completely unprecedented when compared with the characteristics of industrial society, dynamics propelled by both: (1) a psychosocial state of the population no longer content with the consumerist organizational model, which therefore acquires a dynamic potential in the form of expectations; and (2) the combination of the effects of Moore's 'law' and the specificities of IP networks.

But there are a great number of powerful counter-forces opposing these social dynamics, diverting them, turning them against themselves, and models have arisen that could thus be called hyper-consumerist and hyper-consensual, through which consumers self-prescribe their situation, as shown in the work of Marie-Anne Dujarier.[10]

43. Taking care – a new libidinal economy for a new way of life

The characteristics proper to the new technological milieu that forms along with this *technological* protocol of reticulation, which has structural consequences for *social* reticulation, amount to the fact that it is bi-directional and to the fact that it inherently produces and collects a metalanguage of a new kind, through which metadata is formalized, collected and organized: it is the combination of these characteristics that makes possible the constitution of so-called 'social networks'. And the latter are to a large extent the instruments through which pre-digital social relations are being destroyed.

But, if this is the case, it is thanks to true negligence and carelessness on the part of European, national and local public authorities. These reticular technologies are in fact also regional and territorial, and enable local policies to be devised that enhance the relational capacities of a region – and the *capabilities* that this makes possible, in Amartya Sen's sense of this term. The formation of new psychic and collective individuation processes is the development of individual and collective capacities, and we now know how a renewal of economic and political life is conditioned by the reconstitution of such capacities – that is, through the implementation of a genuine de-proletarianization that must be placed on the agenda of national political battles, and through a 'politics of care' that does not reduce care to a question of 'ethics', on the contrary putting it at the heart of a new age of political economy.

The new metalanguage that metadata forms constitutes a new epoch of the grammatization process that globally trans-forms the conditions of transindividuation. A psychic process is translated at the level of a collective individuation through which psychic individuation is marked, inscribed so to speak in the real, and is recognized by other psychic individuals: this work of collective individuation by psychic individuation, and conversely this inscription of collective individuation in psychic individuation, is the process of transindividuation. Now it is precisely this *circuit* formed by the *process* of individuation that can be seen in 'social networks' – however poor they may seem at first sight, just a few years after their appearance.

This is why the dynamic brought about by the reticular IP protocol must be described as the effect of a psychic, collective and technical individuation process of a completely new type. The Simondonian theory of psychosocial individuation is a theory of *relations* in which this individuation is produced *via* the transindividuation process as the formation of circuits that incarnate and activate these relations, and through which the process of co-individuation can be metastabilized.

However poor socio-digital networks mostly seem to be, they now bring together, at lightning speed, hundreds of millions of psychic individuals in a collective individuation process. Political leadership in relation to this fact then becomes an overriding imperative – that is, from the beginning, and over-determining all other imperatives. Taking care of the collective, which is the only worthwhile definition of genuine political action, clearly forms part of this – and in particular taking care of the younger generations, through which future collective forms may be invented, but also through which they may collapse.

I, along with Ars Industrialis, have argued in previous works that the great contemporary techno-industrial alternative is the reconstitution of associated milieus, and the struggle against the dissociation of social milieus induced by generalized proletarian-ization. Associated milieus are relational (and dialogical)[11] strengths, whereas dissociation consists in short-circuiting and bypassing those relations required for the establishing of trans-individuation circuits. Such relations are the condition of forma-tion of trust and fidelity without which no society and no economic system is sustainable.

This context should spur the European Union to elaborate a new industrial model, based on an industrial politics of technolo-gies of spirit – that is, of sublimation – as the only sustainable libidinal economy, and with the goal of producing libidinal *energy*. It is only on this condition that Rifkin's proposal would be capable of supplying a basis for subsistence (and a basis for biopolitics conceived at the level of the biosphere) within a new politics of existence: a *noopolitics* that inverts the fatal logic of psychopower. The genuine question, for Europe as for the rest of the world, is whether it can invent – in dialogue with America and the new major industrialized nations – *a new way of life* where *economiz-ing* means *taking care*.[12]

Part IV

Pharmacology of the Question

6

The Time of the Question

Thus *heimlich* is a word the meaning of which develops in the direction of ambivalence, until it finally coincides with its opposite, *unheimlich*.

Sigmund Freud, 'The Uncanny'

44. Transindividuation as adoption and the time of the question

The *adoption* of a technique or technology by a society, and by an *epoch* of that society, is a phase in a process of collective individuation, which occurs between psychic individuals, and through the mediation of this technique or technology, that is, as individuation that is collective as much as it is psychic, thereby metastabilizing a stage of a transindividuation process. And these are also the conditions of the individuation of the technical system itself, which transforms and metastabilizes itself through this adoption.

This process is the *adoption of a default*, that is, of what any *pharmakon* necessarily induces, namely, the *displacement* of fault (and of the infinite) that we here designate, after reading Freud and Lacan, *das Ding*. A transindividuation process is above all a process of adoption. Nevertheless, as a result of successive stages of grammatization that have made possible the industrialization of production, then of consumption, the transindividuation process as process of adoption has been short-circuited and replaced by a process of adaptation.

This adaptive transindividuation process is formed through short-circuits – whereas adoptive transindividuation forms long circuits. Short-circuits can only result in accidents: they are incapable of generating the necessary, that which is needed (desire and sublimation), from the default (*das Ding*); they are incapable of generating the feeling and the conviction that the default can and must become that which is necessary.

This adaptive process was first of all imposed on those who, as 'producers', were dedicated to trans-forming material: this was the proletarianization that dominated industry in the nineteenth century. Then, in the twentieth century, as all behaviour in every aspect of everyday life came to be controlled, adaptive short-circuits were extended through the proletarianization of the consumer. And finally, as forms of knowledge deriving from noetic life are introduced into computer systems, it is those who work with the mind or spirit who find themselves having to adapt their intellectual activity to the prostheses of cognitive capitalism, their nervous systems setting the parameters of instrumental processes while nevertheless witnessing the reduction and eventually the disappearance of their own noetic activity.

They find their noetic activity depleted because cognitive technologies, developed exclusively in order to increase performance, that is, the speed with which information is handled, are short-circuiting and bypassing their capacity to critique the retentional systems in which these computer systems consist: the time of reflection, which is *the time of the question*, has finally been removed. Having been workers of the spirit, they now find themselves becoming employees of 'cognitive capitalism': no longer workers of the 'spirit of capitalism', but rather employees of a capitalism that has, precisely, lost its spirit, that is, its mind.[1]

45. The possibility of posing questions in the epoch of transformational technologies

The consumerist model only truly developed in Western Europe after the Second World War, and it was not fully globalized until the end of the twentieth century. As for the proletarianization of noetic life that took place over the last three decades, it is the result of a combination of various factors. The two main factors have been: on the one hand, the introduction of digital pharmacology, particularly the fact that the speed of operation has led to short-circuits in the political[2] and noetic[3] spheres; and, on the other hand, the 'conservative revolution' that replaced public authorities with marketing as the means of determining the conditions of adjustment.[4]

It was shown in 'Pharmacology of Capital and the Economy of Contribution'[5] that until the late 1960s the industrial individuation process that led to the systemic disadjustments typical of modern society had been regulated, as the relationship between the technical system and the other social systems – and beyond, or beneath (the psychic systems, biological systems and geographic systems) – by the mediation of public authorities, that is, a political sphere that still constituted a deliberative forum in relation to the technological fate of human societies. This remained the case until the American and British 'conservative revolution', which organized, at a global level, and via financialization, the systematic short-circuiting of politics itself.

As we saw in Chapter 3, the short-circuiting of politics was legitimated by a technological situation such that, 'things being what they are' in the financial sphere, for example, or, in the nuclear sphere, speed – as the performance of information technologies, of missiles, of trading software, or as the effect of the mass media and electronic networks on public opinion and so on, and finally, the overwhelming acceleration of innovation tied to digital technologies and brought about by the exploitation of the micro-electronic potential of matter, and especially silicon – was posited as clear evidence that political time, that is, deliberative time, now finds itself to be de facto obsolete, marketing having taken charge of the adjustments between systems, and having done so by following an adaptive path.

In this way, the short-circuiting of long processes of transindividuation was legitimated – that is, the short-circuiting of adoption. And this situation has led to a short-termism that we are now learning, in a general way, establishes an economy of carelessness and a feeling of general mistrust.

This immense demoralization, expressed in tones that are more apocalyptic every day, is occurring at the same time that, through biotechnology and nanotechnology (which can together be referred to as transformational technologies), a very great bifurcation is taking place in the trajectory of pharmacological being.

Transformational technologies seem in fact to constitute a mutation of technics itself and, according to the thesis supported by several currents of thought that may be referred to together under the general category of 'post-humanism', this amounts to the closure of the history of man – the question of the relation between the technical system, the other social systems and the different organological dimensions, biological systems and including geophysical systems (given that the materials transformed by technical and economic activity are supplied by the geophysical system) being posed here in completely singular and extreme terms.

It is in the context of this demoralization and resulting general mistrust that *hyper-disadjustment* occurs, such that, in the organological transformation process, the level of artificial *organa* forming the technical system seems able to *replace* the other levels: both the level of psychosomatic organs and apparatus, including the genital organs,[6] and the level of organizations and social organisms.[7]

Nevertheless, I do not myself believe that the term 'post-humanism' accurately describes the specificity of the pharmacological turn that transformational technologies obviously constitute. If what must be understood here is the becoming of a life-form that constantly composes with its pharmacological becoming, then to propose that we are entering into a post-humanist age presupposes that we are exiting from an age that can be satisfactorily described by its humanity – and that we know what we are talking about when we use this word.

Nothing is less certain. If we can recognize ourselves as forming a *we*, that is, a unity, within which we are capable of agreement, it is of course true that *we only 'are' in being constantly and always challenged and placed into question* by the mediation of that which, traversing those to whom we give the name 'humans', constitutes their default as well as their excess.

What is called 'man' is apprehended by Heidegger, at the beginning of *Being and Time*, as *Dasein*. And to this being-there, which is also to say, to this ex-sistence, he accords a privilege that is beyond the reach of all other beings. This privilege is that of posing questions: 'This being which we ourselves in each case are and which includes inquiry among the possibilities of its being we formulate terminologically as Da-sein.'[8] I devoted my early works to questioning the way that Heidegger's initial path – of which *Being and Time* was the magisterial peak, but which he abandoned at the end of the 1920s – denies and rejects the pharmacological situation, and in particular the role of tertiary retention in the constitution of the already-there, as well as in its modes of access, that is, in that which, as past, has always already preceded *Dasein*. Despite this, I argue that the *question of the question* that Heidegger poses in §2 as definitional for *Dasein*, and as definitive for any entry into the question of 'the being that we ourselves are', is the only path worthy of question.

At the same time, I suggest that this collective self-designation, as the beings that we ourselves are, must constitute – but at the cost of transformations that will become clearer in what follows – the point of departure for philosophy, if it is to avoid rushing into a humanism that was the sign, in the eyes of Socrates, of the Sophistic evasion of the question of being (that is, for Socrates, the *question*, which always begins thus: '*ti esti?*') by taking man as the measure of all things.

Leaving Heideggerian thought to one side, I propose that the question of the question is that of who, in posing questions, *creates* long circuits and through that *adopts* that which constantly places into question, namely, the *pharmakon*. It is in this 'placing into question' that psychic individuals individuate themselves while being inscribed into a regime of collective individuation where technical individuation operates constantly, and through that so does *das Ding*, as the default that is necessary [*défaut qu'il faut*]: as object of desire.

Adaptation, as a regime of transindividuation that produces short-circuits, is what, insofar as it makes adoption impossible, short-circuits and prevents the possibility of posing questions. Such are the current stakes of the development of industrial technologies of which transformational technologies are the newest stage.

The *first* question is not here that of the advent of a post-humanist age of technics, which autonomizes itself like the grey goo popularized by Eric Drexler,[9] but the completion of a *total proletarianization* implemented according to a purely economic logic that destroys the political sphere, that is, the individuation processes that alone can bring about the adoption of technics, and precisely through the encounter with proletarianization – which is here the accomplishment of the first moment of the *pharmakon*[10] as a short-circuit in transindividuation.

46. The question of the impossibility of posing questions and placing into question before *das unheimlich Ding*

To question is to think for oneself, that is, to accede to the anamnesic dimension of individuation. Here lies the 'possibility of posing questions'. And this is the *first* question, that is, that to which *those questions that arise* for us today are submitted. Such is the question of the question.[11]

If the question of post-humanism *does* seem to arise, however, this is because the question of the question, contrary to what the 'analytic of *Dasein*' proposes as *ontology* (and as the question of *ontological difference*),[12] is itself pre-ceded by the *pharmacological situation* of the 'possibility of posing questions', by the pharmacological situation *as placing in question*.

Indeed, the question has today shown itself to be primordially pharmacological, and the pharmacological situation seems to be the origin of all questions, as the question of the default of origin, and as the question in default of the origin: as a placing in question by the default of origin.

If we are placed above all in the situation that Heidegger assigns to these 'beings that we ourselves are' – namely, noetic beings who *begin* with the *possibility* of the question, this possibility constituting *the noetic itself*, that is, *us*, insofar as we will never cease to question in all circumstances – then it is necessary to ask, at once:

- in what lies this very possibility of *questioning in all circumstances*; and
- whether the *current circumstances* that lead some to speak of post-humanism do not above all lie in the imminence of a *new situation in this respect*, a situation containing the unprecedented risk of *closing the very possibility of the question*.

Perhaps we are in fact confronted, here and now, in this situation sometimes referred to as 'post-human', with what *may* disrupt or interrupt the very possibility of questioning – which obviously does not mean that it is necessary to refer this 'being that we ourselves are' back to the human, nor relate this disruption to 'post-humanity'. To do so would be to miss the entire question: it would be, indeed, to *already* cede the closure of the possibility of questioning.

However things may stand in relation to this disruption of the very possibility of questioning, for Heidegger the question posed by *Dasein* is the question of being. I would like to attempt to preserve this position and this proposition, which characterizes *Dasein* by its possibility of questioning by *originarily* referring the possibility of questioning of 'the being that we ourselves are' to the possibility of being *placed in question precisely in its very possibility of questioning* – and *of being through becoming* such that it *expects to be trans-formed into a future*: such that it expects to be individuated and transindividuated *through adoption*, that is, to be *infinitized*.

The being that we ourselves are would be placed into question by an *impossibility* of questioning due to the initial quivering of every question insofar as it genuinely questions – and that as such puts the being that we ourselves are in *contradiction* with itself, by itself, that is, by and with the other of itself, by and as the very other out of myself that it *becomes* [*devenir*], and sometimes *comes to be* [*advenir*], before what must be called the Thing: *das Ding*.

To specify this more precisely, let us say that questioning would be questioned by the *heteros* that would constitute the hidden face of its *autos* as its *pharmakon*, that is, as that which, pro-jecting outside of itself, ahead of itself, thereby exteriorizing it, may *open the path* of its *becoming* [*devenir*], but may also, at the same time and *in the same stroke*, bar access to its *future* [*avenir*] – its becoming may always dissolve its future.

The placing into question of the possibility of questioning would be the condition of any genuine question. This placing into question begins with the possibility, for the questioned that *could* become the questioning, of being pro-jected into becoming by that which puts into question through the threat of the impossibility of questioning, its pros-thetic pro-jection pre-ceding its possibility of posing questions, as *a kind of in-organic drive*, that is, as an *essentially automatic* situation,[13] and as a placing into question by an *Unheimlichkeit*.

Dasein, if this is what we want to keep calling the being that we ourselves would be, is challenged or called into question by the *pharmacological situation* in which consists its original being-in-default [*être-en-défaut*], that is, its default of origin [*défaut d'origine*]: being-there is questioned and questioning only *insofar as it is prosthetic, and because it is prosthetic*. It is its very prostheticity that projects and places into question *from its very origin*, as default of origin: as *not-yet-being-there*, but *elsewhere*, outside itself, that is, *far* from it, such that it remains always to come.

Given that all prostheticity is pharmacological and that every *pharmakon* is prosthetic (that is, automatic and *unheimlich*), the singularity of the situation that some try to describe as 'post-human' would not derive from any 'technicization' of the being that we ourselves are and will become in questioning – that is, in infinitizing, through adoption, adaptive finitization – since this aforementioned 'questioning-ness' [*questionnance*] would always have been techno-logically and therefore pharmaco-logically given. It would derive on the contrary from a *new pharmacological dimension*, before which or in which every traditional way of questioning would be not only challenged but literally *swept away*.

47. Sin, the scapegoat and the question of God

Prostheticity is this default of origin that almost three thousand years ago took the contradictory name of *original sin*, and more-over also resulted in the 'uncertain origin' of Moses.[14] Prostheticity is the default of origin such that it *opens* the question of the fault of the challenged-being or being-called-into-question [*être-mis-en-*

question], including as the stuttering of Moses, as his faulty pro-
nunciation, or as that of the Ephraimites, as babelization, the
idiomaticity of all languages, and so on. The question of the fault
of this being-called-into-question is then *older* than the question
of its being: it is *older* than the questioning of its being, of its
being-in-question, both as the possibility *and impossibility* of such
a question, opening it *as* the threat and *in* the threat of its closure
(and older than what Heidegger referred to as both the forgetting
of being and *a-letheia*).

It must be asked here what and how Moses, for example, questions and is called into question. It must be asked what and how
the call of Israel and the voice of God, for example, are responses
to, and of, the question. That would require, precisely, passing
through the question of the default of origin that lies hidden
beneath original sin, in which it can already be seen that 'challenging' or 'calling into question', which in this case would be
divine, and which would also be a matter of the *pharmakos*, that
is, of the scapegoat, precedes every question.

That there is always a scapegoat on the horizon of any pharmacological situation, and thus of every possibility of questioning
and being called into question, is that of which religious fanaticism
and all other less visible forms of fundamentalism are effects. And
on this register, secular fundamentalism is no less vulgar than what
it believes itself to be fighting: to make religion the scapegoat for
every evil is to avoid confronting the harsh reality of the contemporary *pharmakon* denied collectively by fundamentalisms and
fanaticisms of every kind, religious as well as secular.[15]

48. The pharmacological challenge as the suspension of the 'understanding that *Dasein* has of its being'

The situation must be called pharmacological precisely in that
prostheticity, in the course of that process of exteriorization that
is hominization – and as incessant compensation for the default
of origin through prostheses that constantly revive and deepen this
fault – is at once that which, at such and such a stage in this
process of exteriorization, interrupts an established possibility
of questioning (what Heidegger called an 'understanding that
Dasein has of its being'), and that which, calling questioning into

question, challenging questioning, thereby revives it in and through another possibility of questioning.

The situation must be called pharmacological in that, at the same time:

- the prostheticity of questioning is poisonous, that is, bars access to the question, not only to *itself*, but to itself-the-*other*, to its becoming itself, to its individuation through the other, that is, through *das Ding* – but more than with Heidegger, I am here speaking with Freud, Lacan and Winnicott;
- this prostheticity is the *remedy* for this poisonousness itself, in fact the *only* remedy, and thus becomes *the very pathway* granting access to this same-other [*autre-même*], insofar as the being that 'we' are become *ourselves* [*nous-mêmes*] (or as one sometimes says in French, '*nous-autres*'), through being *called into question*, becoming a *questioning* being, that is, a questioning *becoming*, that is, ultimately, a questioning *event* [*un advenant questionnant*]: the advening of the question, individuating, through that, becoming-as-future – transforming, sublimating.

49. Again political economy

Such a way of posing the question of the question questions the possibility and the impossibility of a *pharmacology of the question* – and of that which, in a question, in a *true* question, refers not only to astonishment, to *thaumazein*, but to the strange and the disturbing: there is a calling into question through *Unheimlichkeit* – which is pharmacological *just as* the pharmacological is *unheimlich*.

If what calls us into question can also close us off from the question, that is, take us away from every question, turn us thereby into those for whom there no longer are any questions – and thus into those about whom there are no questions – then this does indeed concern a pharmacological question: a *poisonous* (calling into) *question*, that is, self-intoxicating, self-destructive, and which *I believe* can only and must only be called pharmaco-logical, because it can and must nonetheless open the one who is questioned, who is called-into-question, to the at once *heimlich* and *unheimlich* possibility of a question in return, let's say of a *Rückfrage*.

It must open the questioned to the possibility that the question has a curative or therapeutic capacity, that is, to the possibility of a calling into question that takes the question back to its radicality as a question. *So I believe*, just as Deleuze declared that one must 'believe in this world', and just as Nietzsche affirmed the coming of a 'new belief'.

Challenged and called into question by a becoming that is ours (*heimlich*), and that nevertheless escapes us (*unheimlich*), challenged by *that which* pre-cedes 'us' and doubles or redoubles us *in each and every way*, our being-there may become a *no-longer-being-there* [*n'être-plus-là*].

This *no-longer-being-there* proceeds *primordially* from a pharmaco-logical situation in which we become what we are only because we are constantly *called into question*. *But in this time*, faced with *this* new pharmacology that leads some to speak of post-humanism, faced with this new *system* and this new pharmaco-logical *milieu*, we may find ourselves more than ever before projected before and into the becoming of a *no-longer-being-there* without future: not there *ever* again [*plus jamais là*] – *nevermore*.

In the imminence of hyper-interruption, of hyper-epokhality, the current pharmacological becoming bars, or may bar, the possibility of trans-forming this becoming into a future.

Now what is it, fundamentally, that is here being *called into question*? It is *ignorance of the pharmaco-logical situation as such*. And it is, more precisely, a *pharmacology* that can only be *questioning* and *questioned*, as a *pharmacology of the question*, insofar as it is apprehended as a *political economy*.

For in this short-circuiting of every question, where access to the question is barred in principle, and through the fact of this hyper-interruption, through the fact of this epokhal hyper-redoubling, *through the double as such*, and as always through the *unheimlich*,[16] the question arises of an *archi-proletarianization* of the *not-yet-being-there* becoming, therefore, a *no-longer-being-there*.

50.   Not yet there. The height of fault and the two times of the question

This situation of *not-yet-being-there* was stated by Jean Jaurès in the editorial in the first issue of *L'Humanité*, on 18 April 1904 – on which Jacques Derrida commented on 4 March 1999, in the very same newspaper, a newspaper that after the 1920 Tours Congress became the central organ of the French Communist Party: 'Humanity does not exist at all yet or it barely exists.'[17]

If we take this statement seriously, and if we presume that humanity has not begun to exist at some point since 1904, then the question of post-humanism would be completely premature, above all in that it would *not yet* know how to think the question of prematurity, that is, the question of the pharmaco-logy of exteriorization, the question of a kind of *inexistence* of man, an *incompleteness* of man, of man's relation to the incomplete [*inachevé*], that is, to (de)fault, which will have always called the human into question, and doubly so since it is pharmacological, but which, perhaps, here and now, *could* be completed or destroyed [*achever*] (as one says of an injured horse that it had to be destroyed): could *fill in (or make up for) the fault (or defect)*.

This incompleteness is at once Leroi-Gourhan's anthropological question, thought as a process of exteriorization, *and* the philosophical question of individuation as developed by Simondon. To begin by proposing that *there would have been* a humanity, threatened by who knows what 'post' – 'post-humanism' necessarily coming *after* a banal 'humanism' through which, however, one dispenses with having to pose the question and allows oneself in advance not to put anything into question – is to close off, from the outset, what such thoughts put into question, *and the still unrealized possibilities of questioning that they conceal from the perspective of a new critique of political economy.*

For the real question is not post-humanism but hyper-proletarianization.

What questions *can* there be, in general, *after* a pharmacological calling into question? Here the question of the doubly epokhal redoubling arises – here, that is, in the face of that which calls us into question under the premature name of a still immature question, that of 'post-humanism'. This immaturity and its specific prematurity would be the effects of an epokhal redoubling of an undoubtedly unprecedented scope, constituting a boundless and excessive calling into question of this humanity that 'does not exist at all yet or barely exists'.

We must therefore re-examine this redoubled doubling insofar as it is made up of two moments that present themselves in the end as, on the one hand, that of the *challenge or the calling into question*, and, on the other hand, that of the *question itself* – the challenge being the time of *finitization as adaptation*, and the question being the time of *adoption as infinitization*: as sublimation before *das Ding*.

51. Selection criteria and the process of internalization

The primordial prostheticity of the event that we ourselves become, as I attempted to establish in the first volume of *Technics and Time*, is a pharmacological situation that incites a primordial melancholy and hypochondria, of which the devoured liver of Prometheus in chains is the emblem, and this pharmacological situation is the matrix of desire.[18] Never, undoubtedly, has this sorrow [*peine*] – the *sorrow* and *punishment* of those who *hardly* [*à peine*] exist, and who, after the blow from Zeus that punished both Prometheus and mortals,[19] *were sentenced and condemned to toil and hard labour* [*à la peine, c'est-à-dire, condamnés au travail*], to *ponos*, as Jaurès knew better than anyone – never has this sorrow been so deep and so threatening, never has it been so *toxic, that is, disarming*.

The living being that we are, and that we are still becoming, we who would also be animals – a living being that we are and become through what Leroi-Gourhan called the process of exteriorization and hominization – this living being thus becomes *heteronomous* in relation to its own technicity, a heteronomy that means that what is 'proper' to it is also and above all its *impropriety*, that is, its *being-in-default*, its default of origin.

This prosthetic, heteronomous living being *is constantly* and *has forever* been challenged and called into question by a technicity that is *itself perpetually new*. From the moment of its default of origin, this being has continued to develop ways of compensating for the perverse, secondary effects of its primordial technicity. These effects are always *already there before it*, an *inorganic, heimlich* and *unheimlich being-there* that has always already preceded this *as* its past – as that past of which §6 of *Sein und Zeit* states that it has 'always already preceded' *Dasein*, that is, 'us', those who advene [*les advenants*].

We, those who advene, have forever been called into question by *our* technicity or our prostheticity, above all because this technicity, each time new, destroys the arrangements established by the pharmacological becoming of the heteronomous living being that we are constantly becoming, through the invention of configurations that are each time original, and *as such epokhal*, where the heteronomous living being arranges its psychosomatic equipment and social organizations in relation to the technical system that constitutes its milieu, so as to become autonomous *relative to* its *pharmakon*: in essential relation to this *pharmakon*, by adopting it, and by relatively (but never completely) autonomizing itself in relation to its toxic effects.

These epochs emerge from a genealogy that necessitates a general organology, in the context of the occurrence of a process of grammatization. And we must here return to the doubly epokhal redoubling and to its two moments, that is, to the pharmacological character of prostheticity such as it is always concretely expressed by passing through the two moments of the *pharmakon*:

- That through which the appearance of a new *pharmakon* in the technical system modifies this system and thereby *suspends* 'the understanding that being-there has of its being', that is, the circuits of transindividuation that this system had established between the psychosomatic level and the social level of individuation. Let us call this moment the pharmacological challenge, the calling into question of those we have become, where the suspension of circuits of transindividuation, that is, their short-circuit, is what always short-circuits every *possibility* of questioning: this interruption, this suspension, is always a kind of tetany, a kind of para-lysis, an impossibility of analysis, critique, thought, in short, an impossibility of questioning. It is always a poisonous moment, more or less perilous, an inevitable factor in every kind of pain and sorrow.

• That moment through which a *new retentional system* – for the *pharmakon*, being epiphylogenetic, always constitutes a tertiary retention on the basis of which a retentional system is constituted that each time introduces new *selection criteria* – enables the *trans-formation* of this *hypomnesis*, in which Plato located the entire toxicity of the *pharmakon*, into an *anamesis*. Thus, for instance, the geometrical intuition that according to Husserl's late work is grounded in a pharmacology that would be not only 'scriptural' but more generally technical, in this case in the form of techniques of polishing and surveying. All this is well known thanks to Derrida's commentary. But it is, perhaps, *too* well known.

It is only through such a pharmacological inversion, which constitutes the second step of the doubly epokhal redoubling as a therapeutic moment of *melete*, of *epimeleai*, of *skhole*, *otium* and so on, that *new knowledge* occurs, which is also to say, a new experience and a *new work of the question*, a new knowledge of questioning: a knowledge that knows how to pose and adopt new questions (to create new long circuits) through making an effort [*en étant à la peine*], questions that would be worthwhile [*en valent la peine*].

It is also this toil, this effort and this sorrow [*peine*] of which Kant speaks when, in 'On a Recently Prominent Tone of Superiority in Philosophy',[20] he reproaches those whom he accuses of mystagogy of ignoring this *inevitable* toil and sorrow. Derrida's failure to raise this question of *peine* in his commentary on this text[21] amounted to an avoidance of the question of the *work of the spirit*, along with *that of work in general*, and of that *work that is spirit*. *It was, in other words, a way of avoiding the question of the proletarianization of the spirit and of those workers of the spirit.*

All this is of course only valid within what I have described by repeating what *was* there in Derrida, who himself was repeating Leroi-Gourhan, in relation to the consequences of the process of exteriorization, that is, of the *spatialization of time*, of *différance* and grammatization, of the production of tertiary retentions of which the process of grammatization is a specific, belated mode, which gives birth to the West, that is, to what Heidegger believed must be understood as the 'question of being'.

Now, the *new pharmacological moment* brought about by transformational technologies is on this score no doubt quite unprecedented: it may indeed represent a challenge to a *pharmacological framework* that is several million years old, if it is true that what is occurring is no longer a process of prosthetic *exteriorization* so much as a process of prosthetic *internalization*.

52. Processes of internalization and the industrialization of the *pharmakon*

Internalization has always existed, as the internalization of an exteriority not pre-ceded by any interiority, and *therefore not simply an exteriority*. This must be thought with Winnicott as *transitional space* or *potential space*, *neither inside nor outside*, an *object relation* at once founded on and foundering with *das Ding* as default of origin (rather than as 'lack'). It is on the basis of this space that would neither be inside nor outside that internalization will have been possible.[22]

Nevertheless, *internalization itself is today being prostheticized, industrialized and economized according to industrial conditions*, occurring within what must be understood as a libidinal ecology. What ought we think, that is, question, in relation to this unprecedented and blinding situation? What is *called into question* by this prosthetic internalization?

In the preceding chapters, I have tried above all to develop the question of internalization in general and in its numerous modalities, among which what I refer to as proletarianization is the short-circuited mode, the adaptationist, disindividuating mode. I have opposed to the proletarianizing tendency of the *pharmakon* in general, insofar as it constitutes a factor of heteronomy, the analysis of transindividuation in terms of the adoption of the (de)fault – through which it becomes *that which is necessary*, that is, *that which overcomes the opposition between heteronomy and autonomy*.

The process of 'internalization' that in some way comes to invert the process of 'exteriorization' (these terms should be placed within quotes, which also means that *das Ding* is on this side of this opposition since *what* is exteriorized was never preceded by something that would have been 'in the interior') constitutes the *true challenge* and at the same time the *true question*: that of a *new possibility* and a *new necessity of questioning* in and as the default that is necessary [*le défaut qu'il faut*] – that is, finally, a *new way of adopting*.

For what is it to adopt, if not above all to *let oneself be challenged*, and to *individuate oneself* in this challenge, in this being called into question? To individuate oneself: that is, to think, to create new circuits of transindividuation that can be long only because they are, precisely, *open* to question – to the infinite.

Confronted with transformational technologies, this challenge nevertheless creates a pharmacological situation of *absolute urgency*. In this urgent situation, all criteria-production systems – which were always, in the end, organological arrangements of layer upon layer of criteriology, that is, screens that sift and govern the selection process – find themselves challenged, called into question, simultaneously and systemically.

Biotechnologies in their totality enable the trans-formation of those selection criteria of which classical biology was the *descriptive* study, of which agriculture was a *prescriptive* practice, and of which biotechnologies are a total upheaval.

At the same time, gaining access to matter at the nanometric level has brought to light its hypermaterial character[23] and radically trans-formed atomic selection criteria, whereas previously the manipulation of physical matter had been limited to processes of chemical combination. The borders between these fields of selection are now themselves being challenged and called into question, and criteriologies are finding themselves thrown into upheaval thanks to this very fact.

It is even more difficult to identify the right questions that bear, and bring about, this enormous challenge that here *combines* with *primordial melancholy* – challenges are always pharmacologically reactive, and always make us reactive in the Nietzschean-Deleuzian sense – and combines as well with economico-political *interests* that want at all costs to *avoid the question*, either by denying the challenge, or by sensationalizing it in order to create a *smokescreen*, diverting attention from what is genuinely being called into question, from which alone a true question can arise, and as a completely new question.

Post-humanism is such a smokescreen, and it forms a system with this misalliance.

This has led to the paralysis of thinking, and has prevented it from questioning and caused it to give up on itself, that is, on the possibility that what does not yet exist, or barely exists, or hardly exists, may still come to be, by transforming its defect – the other coming from [*pro-venant*] *das Ding* – into that which is necessary [*ce qu'il faut*]. It is here more necessary than ever to pass through Canguilhem, and through his thought of normativity, confronted by the fundamentally pathogenetic character of the *non-inhuman-being* that we sometimes are – precisely when we are normative *insofar as we have the power and are struck by the temptation to 'fall sick'*, and where most of the time we are *inhuman-beings* [*êtrinhumain*].[24]

In *Taking Care of Youth and the Generations*,[25] I tried to show the degree to which Foucault neglected these questions and the pharmacology they require: his archaeology of modern medicine has *nothing* to say about pharmacopoeia in general, still less about the industrialization of pharmacy. But I must again insist that it is only from out of the interior of the industrialization of the *pharmakon* in general, and of the pharmaceutical sector and health in particular, that the 'post-human' can arise as this false question and this new form of deception, a new trap, preventing questioning, that is, preventing us from taking the measure of what is played out in the industrialization of the *pharmakon*.

7

Disposable Children

53. The new scapegoats

We have seen that, generally, a new pharmacological event produces a *primary suspension* that disorients psychosocial individuation by short-circuiting long-established organological programmes, which are thus suspended by this techno-logical *epokhe*. What *Being and Time* called 'the understanding that being-there has of its being' is thus challenged by the *pharmakon*, and as a techno-logical *epokhe* caused by technical individuation, that is, by what Heidegger himself described as a system of references.[1]

The programmatologies through which physiological, technical and social programmes are arranged together, programmes that are established and implemented by physiological, technical and social systems of organs and organizations, constitute a complex and multi-dimensional organological milieu. This milieu is woven by transductive relations knitted together on all three organological levels through the play of the tendencies and counter-tendencies they harbour. And they thus metastabilize, through a horizon of meaning, that 'understanding that being-there has of its being' that constitutes what Simondon named the transindividual.

The advent of a new pharmacological (which is also to say, retentional) order suspends these established programmatologies, and the relations that concretize transindividuality – and we have seen that, as such, it constitutes a pathology, which we can understand as a kind of lesion. The second redoubling, the second-ary *epokhe*, constitutes a new epoch strictly speaking, when the adoption of the *pharmakon* finally generates a therapeutic. This is the process of adoption[2] insofar as it forms a new 'understand-ing by being-there of its being'. Such an understanding is the process of transindividuation through which an epoch unfolds, that is, through which individuation develops at every level into a new pharmacological (which is also to say, retentional) order.

This transindividuation process reconstitutes long circuits on the ruins of those short-circuited, that is, suspended, by the first pharmacological moment, and thereby opposes adaptive models to processes of adoption. What results is not only an understand-ing: it is an affection, a new *pathos*, a *philia*, in short, a libidinal economy, which begins through a dis-economy, and which is the experience of the Thing as the transitional play of tendencies. Here, and through the *pharmakon*, through the generalized tran-sitionality imposed by the pharmacological situation, what is in question as well as full of new questions is the *affect* that is *adop-tion*. Only an affected being can question, which presupposes that it can above all be called into question by its affection.

It is in this sense that I refer[3] to uncontrollable societies of disaf-fected individuals: it is because consumerism has industrially and systemically ruined the process of adoption, that is, of transindi-viduation, by, as we have described, the systemic imposition of short-circuits, in particular via the conservative revolution, that contemporary pharmacology was held at a purely adaptive stage, ruining the possibility of posing questions on the basis of what, in this pharmacology, called the preceding epochs into question, and in particular modernity.

What is referred to as 'postmodernity' is this misery and poverty that is at once symbolic, political, spiritual and now economic – for Europe has discovered with astonishment, and at its core, that the symbolic poverty that is destroying so-called advanced indus-trial societies has now expanded to include economic poverty.

The *enemy of individuation, that is, of the question*, is adapta-tion, whereas the question constitutes the specific modality of existence through which a 'quantum leap in individuation' takes place. The being that we are and that we become is called into question and poses its questions *in a thousand ways* – which are all masks of the Thing that lies behind all transitional objects, those of the child as well as those which overturn an epoch in order to install a new one.[4]

What constitutes here our point of entry into the *political economy of the question*, which is always a *pharmacology of the question*, and as it imposes itself in the context of the industrialization of the *pharmakon*, is the role of marketing – which Heidegger does not examine, and nor does Jonas, Foucault or Derrida, but in relation to which Deleuze introduced the new science of control societies, in lieu and in place of the cybernetics that Heidegger promoted to this rank. Marketing: *confronted with a process of technical internalization* that constitutes an *absolutely singular pharmacological horizon* the stakes of which are literally unprecedented, marketing aims to *impose adaptation in order to short-circuit and bypass adoption, and to do so beyond all measure.*

As for adoption, in the sense given to this word here and also in its everyday sense, a recent disturbing news report provides insight into its contemporary stakes:

When little Artem Justin Hansen, who would turn eight years old the following week, arrived alone on Thursday at Moscow airport, he held in his hands a shocking message: a letter in which his adoptive mother, Tory-Ann Hansen, a thirty-four year old American, stated she was cancelling his adoption and purely and simply sending the boy back to his country of origin!

'I adopted this child, Artem Saveliev on September 29, 2009. This child is mentally unstable.' So said the letter addressed to the Russian Minister of Education, which ended as follows: 'After giving my best to this child, I am sorry to say that for the safety of my family, friends, and myself, I no longer wish to parent this child. As he is a Russian National, I am returning him to your guardianship and would like the adoption disannulled.'

Placed into the care of Russian social services after arrival, Artem had no idea of his adoptive mother's intentions. When he was put aboard the first flight in Tennessee, before changing planes in Washington, Artem believed he was being sent on a tour of his homeland. In his bag, his 'mother' had placed candy, cookies and crayons for the trip. She had even bothered to pay an intermediary she had found on the internet to meet him at the airport.[5]

The most immense question posed by the industrialization of the *pharmakon*, of which the internalization process is the extreme stage and the advent of an incomparable if not radical novelty, is the future of childhood, and not only its future but its very *possibility* – if one believes that childhood is something other than human bondage, something other than an object of sexual consumption, a batch of fresh flesh offered for a polymorphous series of fantasies typical of the contemporary consumer, from the 'mother' who seeks a 'little companion' for her child to the unrepentant paedophile, and that it is, rather, an age at which we must be placed *without condition* under the protection of adults.

Faced with policies that repress children,[6] or the mothers of children,[7] of whom Cosette and her mother are like patrons – policies that are being pursued today especially in France, after having been promoted in the United Kingdom by Tony Blair and his 'third way', where the victims are children, and often also their mothers, put in the position of tormenters, playing the role of scapegoats – how can we not be seized and even choked by this verse from Victor Hugo:

> Alas! How many times must you be told,
> All of you, that it was up to you to lead them,
> That you needed to give them their place in the city;
> That your blindness created theirs;
> From a miserly tutelage, consequences follow,
> And the harm they do to you, you did to them.
> You failed to guide them, to take their hand,
> And to teach them about the shadows and about the true path;
> You have left them caught in the labyrinth.
> They are your nightmare and you are their fear [...].[8]

And how not to weep when reading this passage from Plutarch, who lived close to two thousand years ago in Antiquity, during times thought to be so difficult to endure:

> Nor are we to use living creatures like old shoes or dishes and throw them away when they are worn out or broken with service; but if it were for nothing else, but by way of study and practice in humanity, a man ought always to prehabituate himself in these things to be of a kind and sweet disposition. As to myself, I would

not so much as sell my draught ox on the account of his age, much
less for a small piece of money sell a poor old man, and so chase
him, as it were, from his own country, by turning him [...] out of
the place where he has lived a long while.[9]

54. Exteriorization as exclamation and *différance* as words and gestures

We said that the *secondary suspension* in which consists the curative adoption of a *pharmakon* is the formation of a normative
therapeutic that therefore invents a new *pathos* – another kind of
philia as a new 'form of life' in society – by creating new long
circuits in transindividuation from out of an initial pharmacological shock.

An *epokhe*, as the metastabilization of a transindividuation
process that establishes an 'understanding that being-there has of
its being', is formed via multiple circuits of transindividuation
through which psychic individuals co-individuate and ultimately
transindividuate. This transindividuation is a matter of weaving
transgenerational circuits according to the paths of every form of
knowledge, whether it is mystagogical initiation or apodictic
learning, whereby there occur those moments that Winnicott
called *creative*, that Canguilhem called *normative*, and that Plato
called *anamnesic*. This is a question of anamnesis, of which psychoanalysis will make us aware of a wholly new experience, even
though it was already heralded in Plato's *Symposium*.

In other words, when the secondary suspension takes place, it
tends to create new long processes of transindividuation. This is
contrary to what is provoked by primary suspension, which
bypasses or short-circuits transindividuation, replacing it with
individual, collective and mechanical automatisms, disindividuating psychic individuals and collective individuals who become
reactive, that is, blind, replacing their internalized knowledge
with retentional systems, thereby proletarianizing them.

Contrary to the first pharmacological moment, which above
all constitutes proletarianization, that is, a loss of knowledge (of
all kinds), the transindividuation that is reconstituted in the secondary suspension, that is, in the therapeutic moment of the
pharmakon, consists in creative activity (in Winnicott's terms),

and it is sublimatory in the sense that it generates new forms of knowledge, new long circuits of transindividuation, opened by new questions.

The first loss of knowledge to have been thought as such, and thought as proletarianization, did not affect the know-how [*savoir-faire*] of workers' gestures, nor the *savoir-vivre* of the consumers that we are, or rather that we '*are*' *not*, given that *to be* means to exist, and that to exist is to *know* how to live. The first loss of knowledge to have been thought as such, and thought as proletarianization, was the loss of the knowledge of how to think and theorize that in the eyes of Socrates the *pharmakon* of writing *may* constitute: it is *hypomnesis* as what *above all* discourages, atrophies and ultimately blocks *anamnesis*.[10]

In the second volume of *De la misère symbolique*, however, I argued that noesis is a technesis.[11] This would imply that:

- to receive is to make, that is, there is no perception that is not a production – but *in deferred time*, in the difference operating in the sensorimotor loop;
- perception is a passage to the act and an acting out both by the sensed and the sensing, this passage to the act being therefore an action and not merely a reaction;
- this action – which can itself be 'reactive' – is a *praxis* requiring a *tekhne*.

Given all this, it follows that this *tekhne* is thoroughly pharmacological: it makes possible the creative or normative (that is, individuating) passage to the act *just as much* as the regressive, normalized, adaptive and disindividuating passage to the act. In the latter, the reactive noetic soul regresses to its sensitive level, and proves, most of the time, to be noetic only in potential, and to only be in action sensitively.[12] This must be interpreted as a *regressive movement within libidinal economy to the benefit of the drives and to the detriment of the libido itself* – that is, of that *philia* on to which every noesis opens, given that knowledge is, more than anything, what weaves long circuits of transindividuation, *that is*, transgenerational circuits.

Only *knowledge*, in other words, *insofar as it passes through the experience of that which, not existing, all the more consists,* only this knowledge makes it possible for successive generations to inherit from each other, and to do so without annihilating each other. This latter possibility could eventuate, either by one of them (the adults) descending into perpetual infantilization, or by the other (the children), as may be feared, entering into war with their elders. Such intergenerational war will have its roots in the kinds of reasons outlined in this book, but also in such things as the feeling of younger generations that they ought not be obligated to fund the retirement of their parents, given the degree to which the latter have already mortgaged the futures of their own children.

These are the pharmacological questions posed by Winnicott through clinical analysis of successful and unsuccessful experiences of the transitional object.

'Sensitive' (the word used by Aristotle to qualify *psukhè*) does not mean that the sensible is *opposed* to the intelligible: sensitivity is the regime of individuation specific to the movement of the sensitive soul. But it is also the *in itself* of the noetic soul, to borrow a term from Hegel's interpretation (in *History of Philosophy*)[13] of Aristotle's *On the Soul*. And this *in itself*, if we rethink this term from the perspective of Freud and *das Ding*, is not the instinctual material of the animal's perceptual dynamics but rather the material of the drives, which supplies its dynamism (its *dunamis*) to libidinal energy (*energeia*).

The *per-ception in action* of meaning, conceived in *this* way, sensibly noetic and noetically sensible, is *also* symbolic and technical, wherein the noetic soul is the *différance* of a per-ception that is never a mere *re-ception*, but rather a production that *gives back* and does not merely react, to the extent that it weaves one or more circuits of transindividuation. When I feel or sense something, I ex-press it in some way or other: sooner or later I make it sensible to another – insofar as I sense or feel in a noetic way.

This circuit is that of the exclamation in which desire *consists*, and which *calls into question* the one who exclaims. To exclaim, which is not just to cry – which was the issue in the *Project for a Scientific Psychology* and in *The Ethics of Psychoanalysis*,[14] but on which exclamation builds as *discharge* – is a *gesture*, which may be the articulation of a word or a humiliating slap in the face, or an edifying work [*oeuvre*], or a type of work [*travail*], or any technical exteriorization whatsoever.

A word is above all this exteriority, which re-internalizes itself as a highly artful [*artificieux*], idiomatic default, weaving a process of transindividuation via the tongue within the mouth, through which the default of origin speaks and signifies, while for their part other organs also transindividuate and signify.

55. Cries, crises and critiques of proletarianization

Two things must be added here:

• On the one hand, if this technical *noesis* is pharmacological, which means that exclamation is not just a cry but the initiation of a *différance*, then noesis always presupposes the process of double redoubling on the circuits on which it is inscribed, and such that it opens a *krisis*, a decision, which means that the process of transindividuation is a *critical process*, in that first sense of *krisis* in Hippocrates, where it referred to the moment when the outcome of an illness is decided, which I thus relate back to the question of pathogenetic epokhality typical of the pharmacological-being that we are *in becoming*, that is, typical of a noetic being insofar as it responds, precisely, to a question arising from a challenge.

• On the other hand, something new is occurring today, as an absolutely new challenge, and question, of pharmacological becoming are imposed upon us. This is the challenge and the question of transformational technologies,[15] which must be apprehended above all as the inversion of the process of exteriorization and as the interiorization of technics at, on the one hand, the biological level, and, on the other hand, the physico-chemical level.

How does this call us into question in new and very different ways? It does so, above all, because transformational technologies open possibilities for new types of short-circuits in the process of transindividuation.

But we can say nothing relevant to this possibility and the impossibilities it induces if we fail to understand that these new types of short-circuits are themselves connected to other types of short-circuits that appeared long ago and that have in fact always been contained in the poisonous character of the pharmacology that is all prostheticity.

This obviously does not mean that there is nothing new to think, or that there are no challenges, nothing that would call anything into question. But it does mean that, in order to think this novelty, it will be necessary to think a novelty that has remained unthought, a *longstanding novelty* [*une nouveauté déjà ancienne*] that arose in the nineteenth century as the fate of industrial societies, which is also to say, of globalization, this fate being that of *industrial proletarianization*.

More challenging than proletarianization itself is that which tends to prevent exclamation as the initiation of that *différance* that is a thought (that is, a question) of the proletarianized. It is thereby reduced to a cry, that is, condemned to stupidity.

56. Reproduction, selection and adoption in the epoch of the industrial *pharmakon*: the new critique of life

The true stake of techno-logical interiorization at the biological and physico-chemical levels, for instance in the domain of reproductive technology, and more generally of biotechnologies (without even mentioning here synthetic biology), is the possibility of bypassing [*court-circuiter*] the mother, who becomes a pure belly, either as a producer of eggs to be incubated elsewhere, or as an incubating uterus, that is, as a feminine psychic individual who is thus instrumentalized and proletarianized (the sexed body becoming pure 'labour force') through a division of labour instituting in the world of human life a model founded on the functional opposition between production and consumption.

This is a *proletarianizing* translation of the 'procreatic', such that it is above all and before anything conceived, in all its forms (forms proposed all the more readily after 'ethical' analyses that merely enable us to dispense with thinking what is being called into question, to avoid confronting the new questions that are formed, and through that, the very question of the question – and of its pharmacology), as a *new market*. Such a pharmacological prostheticity of life as interiorization of the technical (de)fault, and as technique for interiorizing a (de)fault that is necessary, can and must, however, be *adopted*. And this adoption must occur as the crossing of a threshold in this history of adoption that pharmacological being has woven from its origin, and as its default of origin.

This is obviously the complete opposite of the way in which this technics of interiorization is being promoted: *the 'socialization' of this transformational technology makes adoption precisely impossible*, being sold as 'medical assistance' by marketing campaigns such as the one seen in the London Underground, trading on progenitive fantasies in the most consumerist way possible – pending the arrival of what Henri Atlan calls the 'artificial uterus'.[16]

The *sterile seed* developed by Delta & Pine Land and promoted by Monsanto, the so-called Terminator seed, bypasses the farmer, who no longer cultivates, but is instead employed (very insecurely) by the agribusiness. The latter, by keeping hold of these transgenic seeds, can *exclude* the farmer from the *selection process* – and it is indeed the question of selection that is raised by this development. Selection, however, is also what occurs in transindividuation in general, either through long circuits as the formation of trans-generational knowledge (which is at bottom always knowing how to question), or through short-circuits as the destruction of knowledge (as proletarianization).

Biotechnological selection can no doubt lead to the problem of eugenics. But well before that, much more insidiously and therefore *much more seriously than that*, there arises the calling into question of the *selectors that we are*, and it arises as the question of a *new proletarianization*.

We are selectors insofar as we can question and therefore respond, that is, transindividuate, and equally, insofar as we raise our children, if we have any, or our students, if we educate any, or minors in general, if we are adults, that is, mature [*majeurs*] and conscious of our responsibilities. These children, these students and these minors question themselves and question us, questions that are posed to, and that impose themselves on, any mother or any father faced with the irreducibility of age-difference and the immense 'out of joint' in which time gives itself and withholds itself in the same stroke – by going through this intergenerational genealogy that tends towards and traverses *das Ding*.

Circuits of transindividuation are above all what form and supply selection criteria, which is also to say, (re)production criteria. In an associated milieu, that is, in a dialogical process, in both Plato's and Bakhtin's sense, this power of selection is thoroughly and organologically *spread* between actors, locutors, and so on. The symbolic is thus inscribed in the systems produced by sexual difference, which condition the relation between the generations, but which can also be technically modified. *Savoir-vivre* consists in socializing a critical system, that is, a capacity to decide (and *all technique and technics* is such a system), for example, in relation to generation(s), where the voluntary termination of pregnancy established a new criteriological age, that is to say, a new critique of life.

When selection is engrammed and automated in programmes that govern retentional systems according to the model of the industrial division of labour, and then of the functional couple producer/consumer as the only model capable of absorbing the costs of techno-capitalist investment, selection becomes dissociation, with all of the resulting effects that have been described in previous works: it is no longer the result of collective individuation, that is, of implementing all the criteria deriving from intergenerational transmission, which is the very process of symbolization, of which the family is one mode and geometry another. And it becomes entropic: it destroys the negentropy that it is precisely the goal of all these criteriologies to create as long circuits of transindividuation.

Today marketing exploits and destroys this intergenerational genealogy: it 'segments' ages into niches and slots. The *ages* of an existence, in their relation to the transitional object, and as the experience of the *pharmakon* par excellence, are epochs of the *pharmakon* during which and through which intergenerational roles are constituted and transmitted. Having become categories targeted by marketing, ages no longer form generations – as if they are a degeneration of (the) generation itself.

Generation, insofar as it is always inherited from genitors and dedicated to engendering, constitutes the elementary basis of transindividuation – in the first place as the transmission of names: that intergenerational *différance* engaged by genitors and their progeny, which can only occur as the legacy of an experience that

must be internalized each time. The relation of care described by
Winnicott is above all this internalization. The latter develops in
a very wide diversity of forms throughout the course of one's
education, which itself does not end with the exit from childhood
– given that the pharmacological being is always having experiences, it is always learning.

Whatever its forms, this learning-internalization is a process
of adoption. As the inverse of this learning and apprenticeship,
and of these adoptions, transmissions and transindividuations,
segmented markets operating via 'age groupings' are promoted
by *pharmaka* submitted to the adaptive processes in which
consumption naturally consists: that which is consumed cannot
be adopted, since on the contrary it must be immediately
disposable.

Hence we are brought into an age of systemic infidelity.

57. For a new politics of adoption

Adoption is the condition of individuation of the pharmacological
being – so that the poison can become a remedy. Adaptation, on
the contrary, which destroys pharmacological knowledge, spreads
toxicity. To adapt is to proletarianize, that is, to deprive of knowledge those who must submit to that to which they are adapting
themselves. The great pharmacological turn of exteriorization-
become-interiorization does not amount to a 'post-humanist'
situation: it constitutes a pharmacological hyper-epokhality that
risks installing a situation of hyper-dissociation, that is, hyper-
proletarianization, and ultimately an unsustainable toxicity.

A process of proletarianization is the destruction of an associated milieu, that is, of a milieu of existence. It is only possible to
exist, for a psychic individual, by contributing to the individuation
of its milieu and by co-individuating with other psychic individuals. This contribution begins with the name given to the newborn,
through which he or she is initiated into a new circuit of intergenerational transindividuation – the condition of all psychic
singularity.

Nomination could and had to refer, for thousands of years, to
a symbolic calendarity prescribing names, to which new names

refer like a spirit. That this calendarity fails when it is replaced by a programme schedule dictates to us the scale of the consumerist system and the immense burden it brings, as well as the necessity of creating a revolution (of declaring what is past: of trans-forming).

To create such a revolution, thus transforming the pharmacological situation – making it pass through the second moment of its *epokhe* – is to invert the situation that leads to the proliferation of situations of infidelity, to abandonments and betrayals of all kinds, from the victims of Monsanto[17] to little Artem, situations that the process of interiorization will not fail to spread if, delivered over to a market imposing the production/consumption model on *all forms of reproduction*, there results a massive proletarianization of interiorization and the disintegration of all forms of adoption. In such conditions, the fate of Artem becomes the norm: such would be the epoch of disposable children.

The question here is a politics of adoption, and this presupposes a pharmacology of adoption. Adoption establishes a relation of fidelity. Fidelity, however, is precisely what defines consumerism insofar as it constitutes a systemic infidelity that, when the hegemony of consumerism reveals its carelessness [*incurie*], installs a situation of mistrust that is generalized and spread as an apocalyptic feeling without God. In such conditions, the harmonious socialization of transformational technologies, appropriate to processes of interiorization belonging to the most recent stage of the *pharmakon*, becomes inconceivable.

Contemporary hyper-epokhality is *therefore* what calls us into question, and above all in the premonition we have of the *immense systemic stupidity* that it is sure to trigger. If it is true that the *generalized* proletarianization that spread at the end of the twentieth century and the beginning of the twenty-first century as a bypassing and short-circuiting not only of producers and consumers deprived of their *savoir-faire* and *savoir-vivre*, but also of theorists and scholars deprived of their theoretical knowledge, thereby becoming proletarians of the spirit supplying their nervous energy to systems that bypass and short-circuit them more and more often, and more and more systemically, then we find ourselves confronted with a situation that absolutely radicalizes the pharmacological question.

58.   Struggling against stupidity

Stupidity [*bêtise*] is what results from the destruction of circuits of transindividuation. This ruin from which nobody escapes causes shame, and it is from out of this shame, engendered by a stupidity that it is a matter of harming,[18] that one begins to think.[19]

Faced with stupidity, the question arises of the second pharmacological moment – which can clearly only be considered through a critique of the first moment, that is, on the condition that a new critique of political economy be constituted, as a new critique of life. From out of this new critique of life, a politics of *adoption*, which is also to say, of a *selection assumed by an associated milieu*, must be constituted as the formation of new types of long circuits of transindividuation, new precisely in that the development of the *pharmakon* and of the turn in pharmacology, and in the pharmacology of the question, may obviously also, as a new horizon of interiorization, intensify rather than short-circuit the adoption process.

We must here pose the question of stupidity as such, that is, the question of the unworthy [*indigne*] and the inhuman. This will be the theme of another work. But I will nevertheless add, provisionally but by way of conclusion, that *bêtise*, which is not merely stupidity (and this is one of the problems that the eponymous work by Avital Ronell[20] poses for a French reader), is what renounces noesis and the noetic. In this respect, stupidity is what opens the inhuman-being [*êtrinhumain*] that we are. The only thing that, at bottom, is worth being lived – in this life that must constantly be critiqued in order for it to be, in fact, worth living – is the struggle against stupidity.[21]

Who or what is the inhuman-being? It is the one incapable of promising – not the one incapable of keeping a promise, but incapable of promising this humanity that does not yet exist. Or barely exists, hardly exists [*ou à peine*]: which only exists by toiling [*à la peine*], that is, on the condition of labouring for its own future. The inhuman-being is incapable of responding to what does not yet exist.

Faced with this, the noetic is what attempts to affirm the non-inhuman-being of what is always too human and more than human, in excess and in default, shall we say, thinking of

Canguilhem: the noetic is as such the being that promises, referred to by Nietzsche as the being capable of standing as guarantor. Such a being is what makes becoming happen [*fait advenir le devenir*] as being – and as always remaining to-come as the highest form of the will to power, capable of 'imprinting on becoming the character of being'.[22]

Notes and References

Introduction

1   This mother, the 'good mother', could clearly also be the father, or some other guardian – and ultimately any benevolent and protective psychic power. And this is the idea behind *The Kid*, in which Chaplin takes on the maternal role to perfection.

Furthermore, in *Taking Care of Youth and the Generations* (Stanford, CA: Stanford University Press, 2010), I drew attention to the fact that Moses and Jesus are adopted children, the former by Jochebed and Amran, the second by Joseph, notwithstanding the fact that in the Koran filiation is defined not by blood but by milk.

This means that care is what makes possible a *process of adoption* – of the child by its mother, and of the transitional object by the mother–child pair, within which the 'mother' is the educator through which is created what Bowlby described as the relation of attachment – thus also the relation between Charlie and the Kid. We shall see in this work, and in particular in Chapters 4 and 8, that care is a process of adoption, and that it is to that extent *precisely not adaptation*. Adaptation is the source of the bad relation to the transitional object, according to Winnicott (see p. 21). We shall also see that it is because the non-inhuman-being is in a thoroughly pharmacological situation that education is always an adoptive relation.

2   '*La vie vaut le coup d'être vécue*': this phrase from Winnicott could also have been translated into French as '*vaut la peine d'être vécue*', 'worth the *effort* of being alive'. And we shall see that pain or effort

is a crucial subject in these matters (see the final part, 'Pharmacology of the Question').

3 In Jacques Derrida, *Dissemination* (Chicago, IL, and London: University of Chicago Press, 1981).

4 And it is necessary to relate this, as we shall see in what follows, to what Freud and Lacan called *das Ding*.

5 This book emerged from a course I gave at Goldsmiths College at the University of London, and from lectures delivered at the invitation of Cambridge, Columbia, Albany, Northwestern and Cardiff universities. I wish to thank Scott Lash, Martin Crowley, Gerald Moore, Benjamin Fong, Mark Taylor, Tom Cohen, Sam Weber, Michael Loriaux and Laurent Milesi for hosting me.

6 A massacre that subsequently took place on 23 March 2002 at the Nanterre town hall.

7 This was Husserl's description of the planet on which we live as non-inhuman-beings. See Edmund Husserl, 'Foundational Investigations of the Phenomenological Origin of the Spatiality of Nature', in *Husserl: Shorter Works* (Notre Dame, IN: University of Notre Dame Press, 1981), p. 228.

Chapter 1   Apocalypse Without God

1 Paul Valéry, 'The Crisis of the Mind', *The Outlook for Intelligence* (Princeton, NJ: Princeton University Press, 1962), p. 23.

2 On this question, see Christian Fauré, Alain Giffard and Bernard Stiegler, *Pour en finir avec la mécroissance. Quelques réflexions d'Ars Industrialis* (Paris: Flammarion, 2009).

3 Valéry, 'The Crisis of the Mind', p. 24, translation modified.

4 'The military crisis may be over. The economic crisis is still with us in all its force. But the intellectual crisis, being more subtle [...] this crisis will hardly allow us to grasp its true extent, its *phase*.' Valéry, 'The Crisis of the Mind', p. 25.

5 Ibid., p. 26.

6 Paul Valéry, 'The European', *History and Politics* (New York: Bollingen, 1962), pp. 307–8.

7 Edmund Husserl, *The Crisis of European Sciences and Transcendental Phenomenology* (Evanston, IL: Northwestern University Press, 1970), pp. 5–6, translation modified.

8 Ibid., p. 6.

9 Ibid., p. 10.

10 Ibid.

11 Valéry, 'Freedom of the Mind', *The Outlook for Intelligence*, p. 186.
12 'The Crisis of the Mind' speaks of a spiritual *physique*.
13 Valéry, 'Freedom of the Mind', p. 191.
14 Ibid., pp. 187–9.
15 I have written on the relations between *otium* and *negotium* – terms that Valéry does not employ – in *The Decadence of Industrial Democracies: Disbelief and Discredit, 1* (Cambridge: Polity, 2011), pp. 131 ff.
16 Valéry, 'Freedom of the Mind', p. 188.
17 Ibid.
18 Ibid., p. 196.
19 Ibid., p. 198.
20 Ibid., pp. 199–200.
21 Ibid., p. 200.
22 *Ars Industrialis* has made the question of the fall of spirit value, of *valeur esprit*, its major object of analysis as well as of struggle – for an industrial politics of technologies of spirit at the service of its re-evaluation. See Ars Industrialis, *Réenchanter le monde* (Paris: Flammarion, 2008).
23 Valéry, 'Freedom of the Mind', p. 201.
24 Sigmund Freud, 'Civilization and Its Discontents', *The Standard Edition of the Complete Psychological Works of Sigmund Freud*, vol. 21 (London: Hogarth Press, 1953–74), p. 92.
25 Ibid., p. 88.
26 Ibid.
27 Ibid., p. 90.
28 Of which I have tried to outline a theory, as the genealogy of the sensible, in *De la misère symbolique 2. La catastrophè du sensible* (Paris: Galilée, 2005).
29 Valéry, 'The European', pp. 308–9.
30 Max Horkheimer and Theodor Adorno, *Dialectic of Enlightenment: Philosophical Fragments* (Stanford, CA: Stanford University Press, 2002).
31 Jürgen Habermas reproduces a similar analysis in his first works, through which he grounds his opposition between language and technics. I have tried to show in *Technics and Time, 1: The Fault of Epimetheus* (Stanford, CA: Stanford University Press, 1998) why this opposition compromises in advance Habermas's political philosophy.
32 See Jürgen Habermas, 'Technology and Science as "Ideology"', *Toward a Rational Society* (Boston, MA: Beacon, 1970), pp. 81–121.

33 I have commented on these passages in *Technics and Time, 1*, pp. 10–13.

34 It is to this immeasurable extent its own remedy, which is something that Plato never thematized, while nevertheless indicating this possibility solely through the fact of presenting writing as a *pharmakon*, whereas Husserl (ultimately), as well as Vernant, Détienne and many others, made it the techno-logical condition of the life of the rational, critical and contradictory spirit.

35 Immanuel Kant, *Critique of Pure Reason* (Hampshire and London: Macmillan, 1929), pp. 164–5.

36 Jacques Derrida, *Edmund Husserl's Origin of Geometry: An Introduction* (Lincoln, NB, and London: University of Nebraska Press, 1989).

37 And the fact that he values such intuitions is what separates Husserl from Kant and brings him closer to Plato.

38 *Translator's note*: 'exteriorization' has mostly been preferred over 'externalization' in order to indicate that when the author deploys this term there is always, in addition to Winnicott, also a reference to André Leroi-Gourhan and to his account of the role of exteriorization in hominization in his magisterial work, *Gesture and Speech* (Cambridge, MA, and London: MIT Press, 1993).

39 I have tried to show this in *Technics and Time, 3: Cinematic Time and the Question of Malaise* (Stanford, CA: Stanford University Press, 2011), pp. 54–7.

40 Edmund Husserl, *The Crisis of European Sciences and Transcendental Phenomenology* (Evanston, IL: Northwestern University Press, 1970).

41 What responds to this question is a kind of transcendental, providing access to archetypes (ideas), but these 'have been given only *indirectly*, at our birth, as an intuiting of copies (*ectypa*)', as Kant says in 'On a Recently Prominent Tone of Superiority in Philosophy', *Theoretical Philosophy After 1781* (Cambridge and New York: Cambridge University Press, 2002), p. 432.

42 I have developed this point in *De la misère symbolique 2. La catastrophè du sensible*, pp. 243 ff.

43 Knowledge as a long circuit of transindividuation is the theme of *Taking Care of Youth and the Generations*.

44 As a result, Heideggerian analyses do not make it possible to think the relation between calculation and the incalculable, determination and the undetermined. See *Technics and Time, 1*, pp. 231 ff.

45 See Bernard Stiegler, *For a New Critique of Political Economy* (Cambridge: Polity, 2010), pp. 29 ff.

46 *Leviticus* XVI: 22.

47 Donald W. Winnicott, *Playing and Reality* (London: Routledge, 1971), p. 3.

48 Ibid., p. 55.

49 Ibid., p. 87.

50 Ibid., pp. 87–8.

51 Ibid., p. 87.

52 I have proposed various sketches of this, notably in *De la misère symbolique 1. L'époque hyperindustrielle* (Paris: Galilée, 2004), and in *The Decadence of Industrial Democracies*, pp. 36–40.

53 I have summarized those points in Marcuse that seem to me the most important and the most problematic, in *The Decadence of Industrial Democracies*.

54 Stiegler, *For a New Critique of Political Economy*, p. 45.

55 But this does not only take hold of the financial system, because it will be imposed on the *totality* of social relations. See ibid., pp. 76 ff., p. 94 and p. 99.

56 See p. 30 and pp. 52–4.

57 See Stiegler, *For a New Critique of Political Economy*, pp. 79 ff.

58 See pp. 34–5 and chapter 4.

59 See Jean-Pierre Vernant, *Myth and Thought among the Greeks* (New York: Zone Books, 2006), ch. 6.

60 It is Gilles Deleuze who reactivates the question of the quasi-cause. Yet Deleuze does not enable us to think the relation of desire and technics, even though Nietzsche opened up this perspective – but this is not how Deleuze will ever have read this – namely, that the pharmaco-logical double of desire and technics, such that the one cannot be found without the other, nor simply with the other, is both apparently very close to, and yet completely lacking (if one can say this), in what Yves Citton finds in his reading of Spinoza and Tarde, 'Les lois de l'imitation des affects', *Spinoza et les sciences sociales* (Paris: Amsterdam, 2008), pp. 69–102.

61 Marie Delcourt, *Héphaïstos ou la légende du magicien* (Paris: Les Belles Lettres, 1982).

62 Jean-Pierre Vernant, 'At Man's Table: Hesiod's Foundation Myth of Sacrifice', in Marcel Detienne and Vernant, *The Cuisine of Sacrifice among the Greeks* (Chicago, IL, and London: University of Chicago Press, 1989), pp. 78–86.

63 Sigmund Freud, 'Mourning and Melancholy', in *The Standard Edition of the Complete Psychological Works of Sigmund Freud*, vol. 14 (London: Hogarth Press, 1957), pp. 237–58.

64 Sigmund Freud, *The Complete Letters of Sigmund Freud to Wilhelm Fliess, 1887–1904* (Cambridge, MA, and London: Harvard University Press, 1985), p. 287.
65 Winnicott, *Playing and Reality*, p. 1.
66 The French translator of Plato, Monique Dixsaut, judiciously translates *me amelesete* – *ameleai* meaning 'carelessness', that is, the opposite of *melete* and *epimeleia* – as 'be not careless' [*ne soyez pas négligents*]. See Platon, *Phédon* (Paris: Flammarion, 1991), p. 309. On the question of *epimeleia*, see Stiegler, *Taking Care of Youth and the Generations*, pp. 135–6.
67 *Phaedo* 118a.
68 Pierre Grimal, *Dictionnaire de la mythologie grecque et romaine* (Paris: PUF, 1963), p. 54. 'The cult of Asclepius [...] developed a genuine school of medicine, the practices of which were mainly magical, although they prepared the advent of more scientific medicine. This art was practiced by Asclepius, or by descendants of Asclepius. The most celebrated is Hippocrates.'

Chapter 2   Pathogenesis, Normativity and the 'Infidelity of the Milieu'

1 It is here necessary to analyse in depth all the links that are woven between consumerist society, that is, the 'American way of life', and *pharmaka* of all kinds – beginning with the consumerist drink par excellence, Coca-Cola, invented in 1886 by a pharmacist.
2 It would be more precise to speak with Simondon of 'metastability'. Canguilhem writes: 'Physiology can do better than search for an objective definition of the normal, [it must] recognize the original normativity of life'. Georges Canguilhem, *The Normal and the Pathological* (New York: Zone Books, 1991), p. 178, translation modified.
3 Ibid., translation modified.
4 Ibid., pp. 200–1.
5 Ibid., pp. 196–7, translation modified.
6 Ibid., p. 197, translation modified.
7 Ibid., p. 198, translation modified.
8 See Stiegler, *For a New Critique of Political Economy*, p. 101.
9 Canguilhem, *The Normal and the Pathological*, p. 200.
10 Ibid., translation modified.
11 Winnicott, *Playing and Reality*, pp. 87 ff.
12 Canguilhem, *The Normal and the Pathological*, p. 200.

13   Ibid.

14   Thérèse Brosse, 'L'énergie consciente, facteur de régulation psycho-
     physiologique', *L'évolution psychiatrique* 1 (1938): 107.

15   This is what *Taking Care of Youth and the Generations* analysed
     as the destruction of maturity, opinion and education by audiences
     and psychotechnologies that capture attention, and it is also what
     For a New Critique of Political Economy analysed as the proletari-
     anization of intellectual work at the heart of so-called cognitive
     capitalism.

16   Stiegler, *Taking Care of Youth and the Generations*, pp. 58–61.

17   See p. 14.

18   Jean-François Lyotard, *The Postmodern Condition: A Report on
     Knowledge* (Minneapolis, MN: University of Minnesota Press,
     1984).

19   See p. 20.

20   Winnicott, *Playing and Reality*, pp. 128–9.

21   Ibid., p. 95.

22   I will return to this primordial question for philosophy in *La
     Technique et le Temps 4. Symboles et diaboles* (forthcoming). That
     philosophy is love (*philein*) of knowledge and that love (*eros*) is the
     experience of dependence affecting the lover, where the loved one
     who structurally escapes this is thus the *heteros* par excellence,
     which psychoanalysis calls the other, but which also presents itself
     fusionally as a double of the *autos*, or more precisely as its 'other
     half' – all this ought to lead to a reading of Plato and of the Ancients
     generally in terms of the question of *logos* as passing through this
     signal transitional experience that is also, for Aristotle, as *philia*,
     the condition of all politics.

23   Bernard Stiegler, *Technics and Time, 2: Disorientation* (Stanford,
     CA: Stanford University Press, 2009), pp. 72 ff., and pp. 95–6.

24   Stiegler, *Technics and Time, 1*, pp. 201–2.

25   I am again taking up the problematic of socio-ethnic programmes,
     explained in *Disorientation* in relation to Leroi-Gourhan, and
     which, insofar as they metastabilize processes of transindividuation,
     form what I call, commenting on Heidegger, an 'already-there'.

26   On this term, see *Technics and Time, 2*, ch. 2.

27   Stiegler, *Technics and Time, 3*, pp. 120–1.

28   Ibid., pp. 87–93.

Chapter 3   Pharmacology of Nuclear Fire, Generalized Automation and Total Proletarianization

1   Prometheus is the figure of precisely this *après-coup*.
2   See p. 123.
3   Stiegler, *Technics and Time*, 2, pp. 122 ff., and *For a New Critique of Political Economy*, p. 47.
4   What is accomplished here in the strategic field is lost in the social field, something I try to describe in *La télécratie contre la démocratie* (Paris: Flammarion, 2006).
5   Paul Virilio, *Speed and Politics: An Essay on Dromology* (New York: Semiotext(e), 1986).
6   Jacques Derrida, 'No Apocalypse, Not Now', *Psyche: Inventions of the Other*, vol. 1 (Stanford, CA: Stanford University Press, 2007), p. 388.
7   Daniel Bensaïd paraphrases thus Books XXI and XIV of *Confessions* in *Marx l'intempestif* (Paris: Fayard, 1995), p. 96.
8   This question of work is also on the horizon, clearly in a wholly other mode, in Kant's text, 'On a Recently Prominent Tone of Superiority in Philosophy', commented on by Derrida in 'Of an Apocalyptic Tone Newly Adopted in Philosophy' (in Harold Coward and Toby Foshay (eds), *Derrida and Negative Theology* (Albany, NY: State University of New York Press, 1992), pp. 25–71), a text which, very strangely, does not raise this theme, which is central. The issue of Kant's discourse is mystagogy – mystagogy, as what makes possible mystagogues such as, according to Kant, certain philosophers, for *believing that it is possible to dispense with work*. In other words, Kant *opposes* work and mystagogy.
       In a forthcoming work (*Mystagogies 1. De l'art et de la littérature*), I attempt to show that, on the contrary, work can only pass through skill [*métier*], that is, *mystery*, and that all genuine work is as such *a kind* of mystagogy. The question of mystery is precisely that of *métier*, that is, of that work that is Kant's theme, notably as that *work of the spirit* that is philosophy, and of its *pharmaka*, and this is a topic that is completely absent from this Derridian deconstruction which nevertheless follows the text of Kant step by step – except for this step.
9   Bensaïd, *Marx l'intempestif*, p. 96. It is regrettable that Bensaïd speaks here of 'particular' time, and that he does not see the abyss that separates the particular from the singular, which he treats almost synonymously.
10   See Ars Industrialis, *Réenchanter le monde*, pp. 48–55.

11 Derrida, 'No Apocalypse, Not Now', p. 390. *Translator's note*: the published English translation of this text differs from the French version, lacking the precise phrase to which Stiegler subsequently draws attention, concerning 'Bergsonian, Husserlian and Heideggerian categories'.

12 This is how Kant characterizes the finitude of the critical subject: contrary to divine understanding, its intuition is not creative but receptive, and the objects of its intuition can only be given through experience.

13 Derrida, 'No Apocalypse, Not Now', pp. 406–7, my emphasis.

14 Ibid., p. 407.

15 In the Bakhtinian sense that also contaminates Platonic dialectic.

16 Heraclitus, fragment 52: 'Time is a child at play, playing backgammon. The royalty is a child's.'

17 In Tom Cohen (ed.), *Jacques Derrida and the Humanities* (Cambridge and New York: Cambridge University Press, 2001).

18 See Jacques Derrida, *Chaque fois unique, la fin du monde* (Paris: Galilée, 2003), p. 9.

19 It is not only criticism, that is, critique according to Kant, that Derrida calls into question, but the critical possibility in its greatest generality, and, in the case of the 'absolute *pharmakon*', this includes 'analysis', 'decomposition' and 'division'. See Derrida, 'No Apocalypse, Not Now', pp. 406–7.

20 Jacques Derrida, 'Letter to a Japanese Friend', in David Wood and Robert Bernasconi (eds), *Derrida and Differance* (Warwick: Parousia Press, 1985), p. 4.

21 Derrida, 'No Apocalypse, Not Now', pp. 406–7.

22 Edmund Husserl, *Ideas: General Introduction to Pure Phenomenology* (New York: Macmillan, 1931), p. 123, translation modified.

23 Jacques Derrida, *Specters of Marx* (New York and London: Routledge, 1994), p. 10.

24 Ibid., p. 189 n. 6.

25 Winnicott, *Playing and Reality*, p. 19.

26 Ibid., p. 118.

27 Ibid., p. 129.

28 Edmund Husserl, 'The Origin of Geometry', in Derrida, *Edmund Husserl's Origin of Geometry: An Introduction*, p. 164.

29 Stiegler, *Technics and Time, 2*, pp. 57–64.

30 Julia Kristeva, *Desire in Language: A Semiotic Approach to Literature and Art* (Oxford: Blackwell, 1980).

31 'If there is an art of photography (beyond that of determined genres, and thus in a quasi-transcendental space), it is found here. Not that

it suspends reference, but that it indefinitely defers a certain type of reality, that of the *perceptible* referent. [...] As for the truth of revelation, it is not only exposed but in the same movement inscribed, situated, adjusted – in the way the developer "reveals" – within the system of the optical apparatus. Within the process of development. Within the functioning of a *techne* whose truth, in turn, etc.' Jacques Derrida, *Right of Inspection* (New York: Monacelli Press, 1998), no page numbers (but cf., *Droit de regards* (Paris: Minuit, 1985), p. xxxv).

32 We will return to this point on pp. 60 ff.
33 See Stiegler, *Taking Care of Youth and the Generations*, p. 124.
34 Adam Smith, *An Inquiry into the Nature and Causes of the Wealth of Nations* (New York: Modern Library, 1937), p. 734.
35 See Stiegler, *For a New Critique of Political Economy*, pp. 76–7.
36 Jacques Derrida, *The Post Card: From Socrates to Freud and Beyond* (Chicago, IL, and London: University of Chicago Press, 1987), p. 351.
37 See Bernard Stiegler, 'To Love, To Love Me, To Love Us: From September 11 to April 21', *Acting Out* (Stanford, CA: Stanford University Press, 2009).
38 Winnicott, *Playing and Reality*, pp. 69–70.
39 *Translator's note*: '*Pensée unique*' is a French term developed as part of a critique of certain political tendencies in France and elsewhere. It refers to the convergence of mainstream political discourse around what is broadly referred to as neoliberalism and to the feeling that there is in fact less and less difference to be found between ostensibly 'opposed' political parties.
40 *Translator's note*: '*charger*', which in French most often means 'to load' or 'to burden', also carries the sense of responsibility or of 'taking care', as, for example, to take care of one's children.
41 See Stiegler, *For a New Critique of Political Economy*, pp. 127 ff.
42 Again, the transitional object is the matrix of a formation as well as of a possible deformation of attention.
43 Plato, *Protagoras* 314a–b.
44 Simone Weil, 'Factory Time', in Barry Castro (ed.), *Business and Society: A Reader in the History, Sociology, and Ethics of Business* (New York and Oxford: Oxford University Press, 1996), p. 92, translation modified. I thank Denis Guénoun for alerting me to this text.
45 Ibid., p. 93, translation modified.
46 Winnicott suggests elsewhere and on many occasions that what is described in the adult as concentration, that is, attentional capacity,

is what is elaborated in the creative relation to the transitional object: 'Milner (1952) relates children's playing to concentration in adults' (*Playing and Reality*, p. 52); 'To get to the idea of playing it is helpful to think of the *preoccupation* that characterizes the playing of a young child. The content does not matter. What matters is the near-withdrawal state, akin to the *concentration* of older children and adults' (p. 69); 'Nevertheless, playing and cultural experience are things that we do value in a special way; these link the past, the present, and the future; *they take up time and space.* They demand and get our concentrated deliberate attention, deliberate but without too much of the deliberateness of trying' (p. 147).

47 Jacques Derrida, *Speech and Phenomena And Other Essays on Husserl's Theory of Signs* (Evanston, IL: Northwestern University Press, 1973).

48 This is what I have tried to show in 'The Magic Skin; or, The Franco-European Accident of Philosophy after Jacques Derrida', *Qui Parle* 18 (2009): 97–110.

49 Stiegler, *La télécratie contre la démocratie*, pp. 247–66.

Chapter 4 The Thing, *Kenosis* and the Power to Infinitize

1 On this subject, see *Les Entretiens du nouveau monde industriel 2009*. Available at: <http://www.iri.centrepompidou.fr/non-classe/entretiens-du-nouveau-monde-industriel/>.

2 Mark C. Taylor, *Errancy: A Postmodern A/Theology* (Chicago, IL, and London: University of Chicago Press, 1984), p. 21.

3 Friedrich Nietzsche, *The Gay Science* (New York: Vintage, 1974), §125.

4 Sigmund Freud, 'Project for a Scientific Psychology', *Standard Edition of the Complete Psychological Works of Sigmund Freud*, vol. 1 (London: Hogarth Press, 1966), pp. 283–397.

5 Jacques Lacan, *The Ethics of Psychoanalysis* (New York: Routledge, 1992).

6 Bernard Baas, *De la chose à l'objet, Jacques Lacan et la traverse de la phénoménologie* (Paris: Peeters & Vrin, 1998).

7 Georges Perec, *Things: A Story of the Sixties*, in *Things: A Story of the Sixties and A Man Asleep* (London: Vintage, 1999).

8 Jean Baudrillard, *The System of Objects* (London and New York: Verso, 1996).

9 Hannah Arendt, *The Human Condition* (Chicago, IL, and London: University of Chicago Press, 1958).

10 Günther Anders, *Die Antiquiertheit des Menschen* (Munich: Beck, 1956), two volumes.

11 Stiegler, *Taking Care of Youth and the Generations*, pp. 12–13.

12 Gregory Bateson, 'The Cybernetics of "Self": A Theory of Alcoholism', *Steps to an Ecology of Mind* (London: Paladin, 1973), pp. 280–308.

13 *Translator's footnote*: 'normative' is intended here in Canguilhem's sense that distinguishes the normative from the normal, where the former is something like a 'metastable' normal, a temporarily apparent norm within an ongoing process of becoming.

14 Simondon, *L'Individuation psychique et collective* (Paris: Aubier, 2007), p. 162, and see my commentary in the preface, p. iv.

15 *Translator's note*: the word here translated as 'facilitations' is *frayages*, which is the French translation of the Freudian term *die Bahnung*, found mainly in the 'Project for a Scientific Psychology' but also in *Beyond the Pleasure Principle*. It is used in relation to the neurological model of psychic functioning and contains the sense of the breaking open of a pathway. Cf., Jean Laplanche and Jean-Bertrand Pontalis, *The Language of Psychoanalysis* (London: Karnac Books, 1988), pp. 157–8.

16 Winnicott, *Playing and Reality*, pp. 128–9.

17 Ibid., p. 95.

18 Edmund Husserl, *Ideas Pertaining to a Pure Phenomenology and to a Phenomenological Philosophy* (Dordrecht: Kluwer, 1989), p. 250.

19 Marcel Mauss, *A General Theory of Magic* (London and New York: Routledge, 1972), pp. 133–4, translation modified.

20 Ibid., p. 134, translation modified.

21 Marcel Mauss, *The Gift* (London: Routledge, 1990), pp. 11–12.

22 Economics speaks of 'diseconomy' to describe the anti-economic effects of negative externalities, that is, the toxicities that are not financially sanctioned and that are therefore not socialized, that is, supported by collectives.

23 Bernard Stiegler, *Pour en finir avec la mécroissance* (Paris: Flammarion, 2009), p. 32; Stiegler, *Constituer l'Europe tome 2. Le motif européen* (Paris: Galilée, 2005), pp. 28 ff.

24 This was recalled by Martin Heidegger in 'Nietzsche's Word: "God Is Dead"', *Off the Beaten Track* (Cambridge and New York: Cambridge University Press, 2002).

25 Bateson, 'The Cybernetics of "Self": A Theory of Alcoholism', *Steps to an Ecology of Mind*, p. 300.

26   Knowledge aims towards a consistence that is infinitive. This infinite motive is what weaves long circuits in transindividuation.
27   These are the stakes of the economy of contribution. See Stiegler, *For a New Critique of Political Economy*, pp. 124–5.

Chapter 5   Economizing Means Taking Care: The Three Limits of Capitalism

1   In the sense given to this term by Alain Mille.
2   See Stiegler, *Pour en finir avec la mécroissance.*
3   Attention understood in this sense is the intentional act par excellence, as passage to the act of intentionality, to the degree that it must be structurally apprehended as aiming at a consistence, that is, at an inexistent, or in other words at an eidetic kernel. This is clearly not at all the sense intended by Husserl in what Natalie Depraz translated as *Phénoménologie de l'attention* (Paris: Vrin, 2009), a work I had not read at the time of writing this chapter.
4   See the website for this institute, available at: <http://criticalclimat-echange.com/>.
5   This was the subject of Alexander Galloway and Eugene Thacker, *The Exploit: A Theory of Networks* (Minneapolis, MN: University of Minnesota Press, 2007).
6   See Stiegler, *For a New Critique of Political Economy*, pp. 73–6.
7   Jeremy Rifkin, *Engager la troisième révolution industrielle, un nouvel ordre du jour énergétique pour l'UE du XXIe siècle* (Paris: Fondation pour l'innovation politique, 2008).
8   Ibid., p. 5. Cf., Jeremy Rifkin, *The Empathic Civilization: The Race to Global Consciousness in a World in Crisis* (Cambridge: Polity, 2009), p. 517.
9   Stiegler, *Pour en finir avec la mécroissance*, ch. 3. It is this approach that drives the activities of the Institut de recherche et d'innovation.
10   Marie-Anne Dujarier, *Le Travail du consommateur* (Paris: La Découverte, 2008).
11   Dialogical in the sense of both Plato and Bakhtin.
12   *Translator's note*: the original French version of this work included a chapter 6 ('Économie de l'incurie') and chapter 7 ('Tendances techniques, organologie generale et puissance publique') that are not included in this English translation, as they have previously been published in *For a New Critique of Political Economy* under the title 'Pharmacology of Capital and Economy of Contribution'. Thus chapters 6 and 7 in this volume are in fact chapters 8 and 9 in the original French publication.

Chapter 6   The Time of the Question

1 On this theme, see Stiegler, *The Lost Spirit of Capitalism: Disbelief and Discredit, 3* (forthcoming).
2 See pp. 37–8.
3 See p. 53.
4 See Stiegler, *For a New Critique of Political Economy*, pp. 96–8.
5 In *For a New Critique of Political Economy*.
6 See pp. 126–7.
7 This hypothesis was examined in the 2008/9 seminar led by Ars Industrialis at the Collège International de Philosophie under the title 'Économie générale et pharmacologie'.
8 Martin Heidegger, *Being and Time* (Albany, NY: SUNY Press, 1996), p. 6.
9 And which is taken up by science fiction, notably in Michael Crichton's *Prey* (New York: HarperCollins, 2002).
10 See pp. 34–5.
11 This was the subject of a work by Derrida, *Of Spirit: Heidegger and the Question*, a citation from which formed the epigraph of Part I of this book. In *Of Spirit*, Derrida on the one hand relates the question of spirit to the question of the question, but on the other hand places in question the question of the question: 'How, without confirming it a priori and circularly, can we *question* this inscription in the structure of the *Fragen* from which *Dasein* will have received, along with its privilege (*Vorrang*), its first, minimal, and most secure determination?' (p. 18). It is precisely this question of the question and of what precedes the question that I am attempting here to explore. And I am attempting to do so insofar as it relates to the question of spirit and conditions the entire question of spirit, precisely as a pharmacology of spirit.
12 In questioning, *Dasein* is the one able to pose the question of being, from which it seems that being cannot be reduced to a being and thus, we might say, is not a thing. But is it not, then, the Thing? I will return to this question in *La Technique et le Temps 5. La guerre des esprits* in examining the way in which Lacan wilfully misreads 'The Thing' (in Martin Heidegger, *Poetry, Language, Thought* (New York: Harper, 1975), pp. 163–86) in his interpretation of Freud's *das Ding*. And, as for Heidegger's highly mystagogical text, it would be necessary to show how the two extracts below could be inverted: 'What, then, is the thing as thing, that its essential nature has never yet been able to appear? Has the thing never yet come near enough for man to learn how to attend sufficiently to the thing as thing?

What is nearness?' (p. 171). 'To be sure, the Old High German word *thing* means a gathering, and specifically a gathering to deliberate on a matter under discussion, a contested matter. In consequence, the Old German words *thing* and *dinc* become the names for an affair or matter of pertinence. They denote anything that in any way bears upon men, concerns them, and that accordingly is a matter for discourse [or questioning]' (p. 174).

13   On the question of the automaticity of technics, if not of the *pharmakon*, see David Wills, *Dorsality: Thinking Back Through Technology and Politics* (Minneapolis, MN: University of Minnesota Press, 2008).

14   Thomas Mann, *The Tables of the Law* (London: Haus, 2010), p. 14, translation modified. (*Translator's note*: the original German is *fragliche*, rendered in Marion Faber and Thomas Lehmann's recent English translation as 'problematic', whereas the French translation cited by Stiegler refers to *l'origine douteuse*.)

15   If the Third Republic had to battle against the toxic control exerted by the Church on souls through a politics that can only be understood in relation to the struggles of the Reformation and Counter-Reformation, the poisoners today mostly lie on the other side.

16   Freud introduced the question of the *unheimlich* through the figure of the double, Olympia, in Hoffmann's 'The Sandman'. See Freud, 'The Uncanny'.

17   Jean Jaurès, cited in Jacques Derrida, 'My Sunday "Humanities"', *Paper Machine* (Stanford, CA: Stanford University Press, 2005), p. 100. I thank Charles Sylvestre for alerting me to this text delivered by Derrida in 1999 at the Fête de l'Humanité.

18   See p. 24. We must here cite, in relation to desire, two analyses by Dominique Lecourt of technics in the epoch of the 'post-human' fantasy: 'A "decoupling" [*décrochage*] occurs that makes the human being a singular animal; we imagine that through a very gradual process, it becomes the animal that we are. The human is the animal who is not adapted to its milieu, contrary to what is implied by a vocabulary of Lamarckian origin, used and abused by educational psychology; the human is on the contrary the one who actively adapts his environment to his desires, which prove to be as insatiable as they are diverse. The essence of technics, if one may speak in these terms, lies here: through it, human beings detach themselves from their animality, which remains theirs not as a being of needs, nor as a being having reason, but as a desiring being' (*Humain*,

posthumain: la technique et la vie (Paris: PUF, 2003), p. 43). 'Would there not be another path, that of normative invention? This path amounts not to a recourse to the super-human, nor is it to succumb to the vertigo of the post-human, but rather to build upon one of the preeminent qualities of the human being: its capacity to constantly reinvent its way of being human on the basis of the achievements and realizations of its own genius. In the fifteenth century Jean Pic de La Mirandole referred to this quality as "human dignity" – that which creates its own value' (ibid., p. 48). It is tempting here to return – in the face of this *question of dignity* – to Valéry, and to spirit value [*valeur esprit*]. But it would then be necessary to again pose the question of the organology of spirit which, pharmacologically, is also what constantly inverts itself into its opposite and, becoming poison, engenders the *indignity of the inhuman*, and of what I have attempted to refer to in *Taking Care of Youth and the Generations* (§53) as *inhuman-being* [*êtrinhumain*]. For such is the being of desire: inhabited by the inhuman yet all too human drives – those about which we indulgently say, 'it's human…' The normative inventiveness that I am myself advocating presupposes a pharmacological critique that, as we have seen, requires a new critique of political economy. It cannot ignore the irreducible ambiguity of that *pharmakon* that is all technics, and the potential indignity contained in *every* aspiration to dignity.

19 Vernant, 'At Man's Table', *The Cuisine of Sacrifice among the Greeks*, pp. 35–6.

20 '[D]iscursive understanding must employ much labor on resolving and again com-pounding its concepts according to principles, and toil up many steps to make advances in knowledge' (Kant, 'On a Recently Prominent Tone of Superiority in Philosophy', *Theoretical Philosophy after 1781*, p. 431). In *Mystagogies 1* (forthcoming), I try to show that Kant, in his thought of aesthetic judgment, struggling here against a mystagogical penchant of philosophy that, out of laziness, cannot escape mystification, nevertheless himself poses that the experience of beauty and the reflective judgment that is its expression are irreducibly mystagogical.

21 See p. 141, n.8.

22 See pp. 20–1.

23 On this notion, see Bernard Stiegler, *Économie de l'hypermatériel et psychopouvoir* (Paris: Mille et une nuits, 2008).

24 Stiegler, *Taking Care of Youth and the Generations*, §52.

25. Ibid., pp. 124ff.

Chapter 7   Disposable Children

1 Heidegger, *Being and Time*, §17.
2 This presupposes the explanations provided in *Technics and Time, 3*, ch. 3.
3 In Bernard Stiegler, *Uncontrollable Societies of Disaffected Individuals: Disbelief and Discredit, 2* (Cambridge: Polity, 2012).
4 It is as a relation to the *pharmakon* that a question can impose itself and pose itself, and this position of a question is above all an object relation, where the privilege that we accord to the verbal relation lies in the objectification that takes place with the written word, discretized and spatialized through grammatization – a privilege that, in societies of *mana* and *hau*, is still largely distributed among things, of which Perec's *Things* announces the obsolescent and essentially disposable fate.
5 'Une Américaine renvoie en Russie l'enfant qu'elle avait adopté', *Le Parisien*, available at: <http://www.leparisien.fr/faits-divers/une-americaine-renvoie-en-russie-l-enfant-qu-elle-avait-adopte-10-04-2010-880860.php>.
6 On the criminalization of youth and children, see *Taking Care of Youth and the Generations*, ch. 1, or, on keeping files on three-year-old children, see *Uncontrollable Societies of Disaffected Individuals* and http://www.pasde0deconduite.org/appel/, or the policies penalizing families whose children are absent from school, and so on. The *États généreux pour l'enfance* is dedicated to analysing and denouncing this literally shameful politics: 'The "General State of Childhood" released by the Secretary of State for the Family will not lead to the improvement of the situation of children. Maintaining current policies, it proceeds from a logic that is detrimental to children and for the whole of society: presenting youth as a problem for society; making families solely responsible for the difficulties of their children; claiming that restraining children, isolating those that cause problems, and controlling behaviour, will protect society. In the face of this general state [*états generaux*] of children, our Generous State [*États génerEux*] declares grievances! Close to eighty organizations – collectives, associations, unions – have combined to launch *États génerEux pour l'enfance* and provide a comprehensive review of government policies concerning children. They combined their views into a *List of grievances in support of children*. This laid out the basis of an overall, positive national policy FOR children, representing the interests of children and respecting them and their families, while listening to the professionals and organizations that accompany them.'

7 For instance, the politics of control implemented in the United Kingdom by Tony Blair and his 'New Labour' against single mothers whose children are a priori considered to be potential delinquents – as if this were not so for the whole world, from Sarkozy to the Pope, and passing through Madoff and his 'victims'.

8 Victor Hugo, 'À ceux qu'on foule aux pieds' ['To those trampled underfoot'], *L'Année terrible*, 1872. I would like to thank Robin Renucci, who brought this poem to my attention.

9 Plutarch, 'Marcus Cato', *Plutarch's Lives: The Translation Called Dryden's* (New York: Bigelow, Brown & Co., no date), p. 355.

10 Stiegler, *For a New Critique of Political Economy*, pp. 29 ff.

11 Stiegler, *De la misère symbolique 2*, pp. 61–71.

12 Stiegler, *The Decadence of Industrial Democracies*, ch. 4.

13 Georg Wilhelm Friedrich Hegel, *Lectures on the History of Philosophy, 1825–6. Volume II: Greek Philosophy* (Oxford: Oxford University Press, 2006).

14 Sigmund Freud, 'Project for a Scientific Psychology', *Standard Edition of the Complete Psychological Works of Sigmund Freud*, vol. 1 (London: Hogarth Press, 1966), pp. 283–397; Jacques Lacan, *The Ethics of Psychoanalysis* (New York: Routledge, 1992).

15 This will be one of the subjects discussed in Stiegler, *Prendre soin 2*.

16 Henri Atlan, *L'Utérus artificiel* (Paris: Seuil, 2007).

17 According to the 25 May 2010 issue of the Canadian newspaper *Le Devoir*, two hundred thousand small Indian cotton growers have committed suicide in the east of Maharashtra since 1997: 'Fertilizers have depleted the soil, which provides less and less, the price of cotton has fallen, and it becomes necessary to take on debt in an unsustainable way in order to purchase every year the genetically modified seeds that do not occur naturally.'

18 *Translator's note:* the author is here referring to Nietzsche's discussion, in *The Gay Science*, of 'harming stupidity' (see §328).

19 I have begun to explore these questions in *Uncontrollable Societies of Disaffected Individuals*, p. 24, and in *Constituer l'Europe 1: Dans un monde sans vergogne* (Paris: Galilée, 2005).

20 Avital Ronell, *Stupidity* (Champaign, IL: University of Illinois Press, 2002).

21 On this point I diverge completely from the analyses of Avital Ronell.

22 Friedrich Nietzsche, *The Will to Power* (New York: Vintage Books, 1967), §617, translation modified.

Index

man
  capable of variation 28–9
  as *Dasein* 105, 107–9, 114
  humanity of 104–6, 112–13,
    122–3, 132–3
  incapable of taking care of
    himself or others 32
  as a prosthetic god 14
mana 73
Manichaeism 77
Maoris 73
Marcuse, Herbert 22
marketing 10, 31, 32, 63, 82, 89
  by age-grouping 129–30
  socialization via 74, 84, 90,
    94, 95, 103, 121
  of transformational technology
    127–30
Marx, Karl 39, 87
Marxism 39
mathesis 18, 19
matter 103, 117
maturity (*majorité*) 15, 42, 128
Mauss, Marcel 72
meaning
  and emotion 67
  production of 67–8, 85–6, 95
melancholy 3, 14–15, 25, 43,
    113, 117
Melanesians 73
melete 34, 115
memory
  anamnesic 2, 18
  artificial (hypomnesic) 2, 18,
    25
  epigenetic 65
  industrialization of psychic and
    collective 83
  phylogenetic 65
  as secondary retention 85–6
  technical 65
  transcendental 18, 19

metadata 95, 96–7
metalanguage 96–7
metaphysics 50
Meyer, Leonard 85
milieu
  associated 97–8, 119, 129,
    130–1, 132–3
  'associated techno-geographic'
    (Simondon) 95–6
  audiovisual pharmacological
    69, 72, 111
  digital 75, 76
  epiphylogenetic 65–6
  hyper-mediatized and
    hallucinatory 66–7
  'infidelity of the' 27–36, 53,
    65
  'preindividual' (Simondon) 48
  for relations of fidelity 62
  transitional 78, 84, 114
military 37–9
minds, control of 15–16
miscreance (*mécréance*) 59, 95
misgrowth (*mécroissance*) 90, 95
monotheism 77
Monsanto 128, 131
moral consciousness 23
Moses 108–9
mother
  bypassing the 127
  care by the 1–4, 20–2
motives 23, 93–4
  pure and infinite 34
motricity 66, 69
mystagogy 115

names 129–31
nanotechnology 104, 117
nationalism 30
needs, hierarchy of 13–14
negotium, and *otium* 13, 50, 53,
    60–1

Made in the USA
Monee, IL
06 October 2021

79508440R00098